Modellers' & Enthusiasts' Guide to
THE SOMERSET & DORSET LINE

Modellers' & Enthusiasts' Guide to THE SOMERSET & DORSET LINE

Brian Macdermott

Patrick Stephens, Cambridge

Title page *4F 0-6-0, 44557, leaves Midford on October 5 1957 with a Bath to Templecombe train formed by Maunsell set 399 and a strengthening coach* (Ivo Peters).

© Brian Macdermott and Patrick Stephens Ltd 1982

All rights reserved. No part of this publication may be reproduced, stored in a retrieval system, or transmitted, in any form or by any means, electronic, mechanical, photocopying, recording or otherwise, without prior permission in writing from Patrick Stephens Limited.

First published in 1982

British Library Cataloguing in Publication Data
Macdermott, Brian
   Modellers' and enthusiasts' guide to the
   Somerset and Dorset Line.
   1. Somerset and Dorset Joint Railway—History
   I. Title
   385'.2'09423   HE3020.S/

ISBN 0-85059-586-X

Photoset in 10 pt Plantin by Manuset Limited, Baldock, Herts. Printed in Great Britain on 100 gsm Fineblade coated cartridge, and bound, by Woolnough Bookbinding, Wellingborough, Northants, for the publishers, Patrick Stephens Limited, Bar Hill, Cambridge, CB3 8EL, England.

Contents

	Introduction	**6**
Chapter 1	**Some background notes**	**9**
Chapter 2	**Bath (Green Park)**	
	A general description . . . Freight and other non-passenger carrying trains . . . Local service to Bristol Temple Meads . . . Through service, Bristol Temple Meads to Bournemouth West . . . Local service to Templecombe . . . Local service to Binegar . . . The *Pines Express* . . . Summer Saturdays . . . Special trains . . . The model	**11**
Chapter 3	**Lyncombe Vale**	**42**
Chapter 4	**Midford**	**46**
Chapter 5	**Radstock**	**55**
Chapter 6	**Midsomer Norton and Norton Hill Colliery**	**58**
Chapter 7	**Binegar**	**64**
Chapter 8	**Evercreech Junction and 'the branch' services**	**68**
Chapter 9	**Templecombe**	**82**
Chapter 10	**The rest of the line to Bournemouth West**	**88**
Chapter 11	**Conclusions**	**90**
	Appendices	**92**

Introduction

The Somerset and Dorset line has often been described as a unique stretch of railway. This book about the line has been written to appeal to both railway modeller and railway enthusiast alike. The period covered is from 1950 up to closure of the line in March 1966. Starting with a description of the Midland station at Bath, details are given of the day-to-day workings of the station, its services and types of motive power. Interwoven with the text, ways and means have been suggested whereby the information can be translated into model form suitable for the individual modeller or club. The same treatment is given to various interesting locations along the route, ranging from the tranquil surroundings of the single line stretch of track between Devonshire and Combe Down tunnels, to the busy scenes which were once a feature at Bath (Green Park) and Evercreech Junction. The photographs have been chosen to show not only the diversity of motive power and rolling stock, but also to include as much modelling detail as possible, such as signals, signal boxes, goods sheds and station buildings. The work is intended to give as complete a picture of the line as possible for the enthusiast and to provide inspiration for the modeller. A chapter is included to show where further or more specialised information can be found and appendices give detailed information on the working timetables at various stations.

How many times have you read in the model railway press that a club or individual has modelled 'a fictitious station (or area) where all our favourite locos and rolling stock from all four main BR regions could be seen working together'? At Bath (Green Park), however, fiction became fact on several summer Saturdays in the 1950s and early 1960s, when all six BR regions were represented. The rest of the line down to Bournemouth West sported examples of Western, London Midland and Southern Region locos and rolling stock on a regular daily basis from 1958 onwards. Anything from a Jinty running light engine to a 7F 2-8-0 piloting a 9F 2-10-0 on the *Pines Express* might be seen, although it should be noted that the latter combination was a 'one off'.

An attempt has been made to provide a complete description of the line so that the modeller can make up his own mind as to what is worth modelling and what isn't. Exact scale drawings of buildings have deliberately been excluded as discussions with modellers have revealed that the majority are forced into a situation of compromise when it comes to space and finance. Indeed, to make an exact scale model of, say, a goods shed and then put it on a model which is possibly half scale size is simply a recipe for disaster, or at least disillusionment and subsequent loss of interest. Therefore, the photographs and text are presented in such a way that most of the information is there, but it is up to the reader to interpret it in his or her own way. Beauty is in the eye of the beholder, as they say. A note of warning; all references to the working timetable *must be treated as a guideline only*. There were many things which could alter the day-to-day running of the line, such as late running of connecting services, loco failures, Bank Holiday extras and so on.

The track plans shown throughout the book are based on prototype drawings but have been modified to suit a room measuring approximately 12 feet by 8 feet when modelling in 00 gauge. (The only exception to this is the plan for Evercreech Junction, which

Introduction

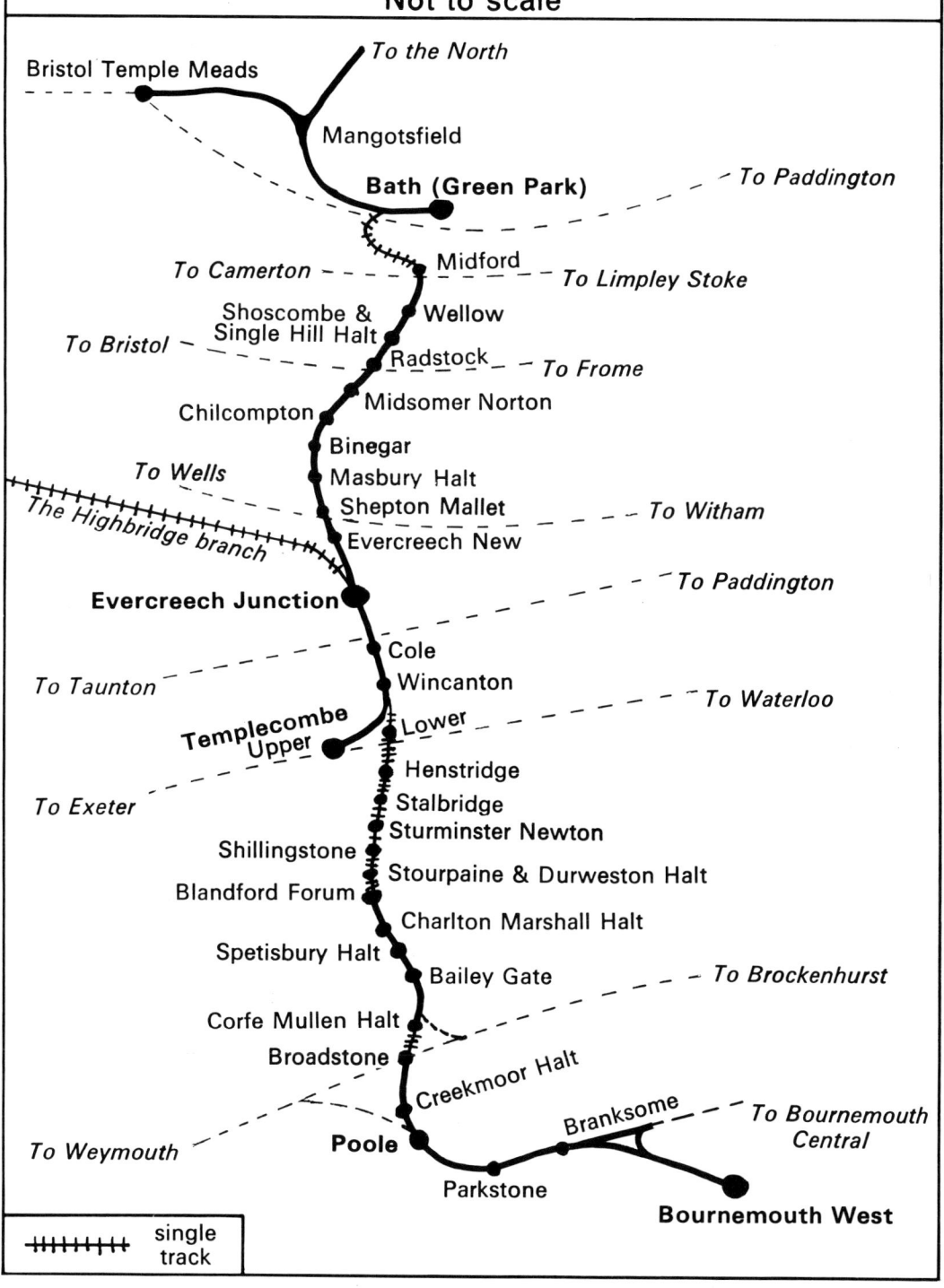

has been designed for a 20 feet by 12 feet room in 00 gauge). The size chosen is believed to represent a reasonable average of sizes available to the modeller. Most schemes can be enlarged to fit a garage measuring 16 feet by 8 feet or, conversely, be contracted to fit an 8 feet by 6 feet 'spare' room, particularly in N gauge. The plans should only be treated as a suggestion of what can be done. However, they have all been drawn with one common aim in mind: to enable the modeller to recreate the essential day-to-day workings of the original as closely as possible. My experience with railway modelling over the past few years has shown me that a model based on a prototype will probably afford more pleasure to the operator than one based on a fictitious location.

Chapter 1

Some background notes

Depending on one's outlook or loyalties the initials S & D stood for 'Slow and Dirty' or 'Swift and Delightful'. Modellers and enthusiasts would no doubt choose the latter description with all the pleasures the S & D afforded. The line and all its eccentricities became a mecca for enthusiasts, particularly in its final years. Possibly there is more interest in the S & D today, more than 15 years after closure, than there ever has been. Very little remains as evidence that a railway line ever went through some towns and villages on the route. Station buildings have been demolished or converted for other purposes, bridges have been dismantled and cuttings filled in by farmers to increase their land. Nonetheless, the memory remains, having been perpetuated on film by many well known people, such as Ivo Peters, Derek Cross and R.E. Toop. By the way, keep an eye out for Ivo Peters' car in his photographs. It has a tendency to pop up rather like Alfred Hitchcock used to do in his many films!

The S & D formed a cross-country link between the south coast and the Midlands. The post-war passenger traffic over the line reached a peak in the early and mid-1950s with many holiday trains running between the popular resort of Bournemouth and the industrial towns of the Midlands and north of England. Coal from the Somerset coalfields and Mendip stone accounted for a healthy flow of freight trains with one of the well known 7F 2-8-0s usually at the head. The busiest section of the S & D was the northern half between Bath and Templecombe, with most freight trains plying between Bath and Evercreech Junction. Freight traffic thinned out between Templecombe and Bournemouth West. For that reason the main content of this book concerns the northern half of the line. The emphasis is placed on the operation of Bath (Green Park) with its freight services to Westerleigh, Avonmouth, Birmingham and Evercreech Junction, together with passenger services to Bristol Temple Meads (also St Philip's in the early 1950s), Templecombe and Bournemouth West, as well as the holiday express destinations.

Although the Southern Region operated the S & D line between January 1950 and February 1 1958, everything north of Cole came under the Western Region on a commercial basis. Locomotive stock was loaned to the Southern Region by the London Midland Region until 1953, when those engines were formally transferred to the Southern's stock list. The important point about 1958 is that from February 1 the Western Region gained not only control of the S & D motive power depots, but virtual complete commercial control of the line and was therefore able to dictate the level of traffic. Bath's shed code changed from 71G to 82F and Templecombe's from 71H to 82G. Slowly, but very surely, changes were implemented so that by the end of the summer service of 1962 all through expresses from and to the north were re-routed. The *Pines Express*, the line's premier train, was included in these re-routings. Some say that these changes came about as a form of revenge dating back to S & DJR and GWR days when, apparently, the two companies had something of a *contre-temps*. The winter service of 1962 saw the line reduced to a purely local service. For a time during 1963, 92220, *Evening Star*, spent her days plying back and forth with three coach locals. A short reprieve from the axe came in early 1966 as arrangements for replacement transport services could not be agreed satisfactorily. All services came to an end in March of that year.

One of the main causes for closure of the line was, in modern terms, the uneconomic way trains needed to be piloted over the Mendips and then, for the remainder of the journey, have another loco attached to them at Bath. It was hoped that the powerful 9Fs would solve the problem of piloting. With the advent of the longer and heavier BR coaching stock on the *Pines Express* and the amount of effort needed by the loco's fireman on a daily basis on a 9F, pilots were again found necessary. The 9Fs did, however, handle most of the Saturday-only trains unaided. It is sad to note that the sight of two locos working hard together, which was so enjoyed by the enthusiast and photographer, was to be a major contributing factor in the demise of the line.

Over the years the working timetables altered very little. Indeed, the equivalent of the 1961 2.40 am Freight and Mail was noted in the working timetable for 1895, albeit with a departure time just 10 minutes later. A transcription of the 1961 working timetable has been included in the appendices. It is intended to use this as a reference as most times quoted throughout the text are based on it. As stated in the introduction these times should be used as a guideline to what was planned to happen, not what actually did happen. For example, the insertion of extra trains often resulted in some retiming of the existing ones. Freight trains were frequently despatched as soon as they were ready to go and that could sometimes be as much as an hour before booked time. Similarly, where reference is made to a particular loco roster or unusual shunting operation, it must be remembered that various circumstances could change the way things were done over a period of time. Accurate dates are used wherever possible. In the absence of dates, general items of information are given which can be put to good use on a model to add interest to its operation.

Chapter 2

Bath (Green Park)

A general description

To divide the S & D into orderly portions for description is extremely difficult. There are so many overlaps in the way things happened that precise dividing lines are not always apparent. Therefore, under this general heading of Bath (Green Park), an outline of all the services which worked into the station has been given. Even this is not an easy task to perform as there were many variations on a theme, as will be pointed out, but, I suppose, that is what Bath and the S & D was all about. Without all the mystery and intrigue over what type of loco would be coming along next there would be no story to tell. (An article concerning the history of Bath (Green Park) appears in the *Railway Magazine* of June 1980, written by Mike Arlett.)

Looking at the outside of the station as a passenger in the 1950s you would have seen that the buildings fitted in well with the surroundings, although the passing of time took its toll with the stonework. The whole structure was 'Georgian' in appearance, matching the style of many other buildings in that elegant city. A glazed canopy over part of the forecourt gave covered access to the booking hall which in turn led to a concourse at the buffer stop end of the two platforms. Platform and train indicator boards were in the form of interchangeable arms. Various offices and passenger facilities were located on both platforms, extending about a third of the way down. The overall roof covered wooden platforms for half of the platform length. This delightful structure would certainly make a most attractive model. Prior to the Second World War it was fully glazed, but during bombing raids on the city most of it was blasted out and never replaced. (There's a good excuse for an unfinished model!) The cavernous nature of the station accentuated the sounds made by the wheeltapper going about his business. When the Western Region gained control in 1958 the station was repainted in chocolate and cream where appropriate.

A simplified sketch plan of the track layout up to Bath Junction has been included to which reference should be made. The station had two platforms which were used as necessary for arrival or departure although there was a normal pattern of events when things were running smoothly. (More of that will be found in the following sub-sections of this chapter.) The shorter platform on the north side of the station could handle trains of eight coaches plus an engine. The longer platform on the south side could handle nine coaches plus an engine. (Railwaymen usually referred to the platforms as north or south respectively as opposed to any other description which could be applied, such as short, long, arrival, departure, etc.) The holiday expresses were regularly loaded to 10 or 11 coaches, so 'overhanging' was not an uncommon sight. To this effect the sectional appendix to the working timetable stated that guards of over-length trains should go through the rear vehicles and advise passengers intending to alight at Bath to proceed along the train as far as may be necessary.

Adjacent to the north platform was a run-round facility controlled from a small ground frame. This road was also used for stock storage, the short spur from the cross-over to the buffer stop holding two coaches. The road

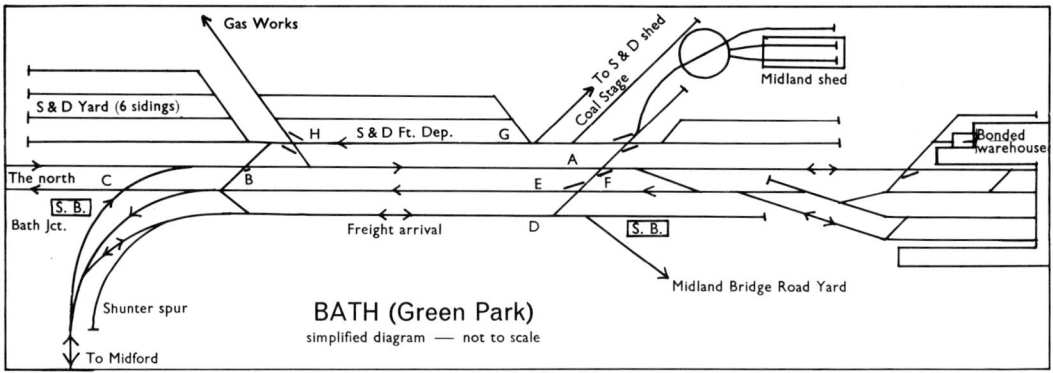

BATH (Green Park)
simplified diagram — not to scale

adjacent to the south platform was a dead end and was used for holding empty stock. A gas tanker invariably sat up against the stops of this road during the summer service. Water taps were situated alongside the central road and the carriage siding, a small item which I cannot recall ever having seen on a model. The wooden surrounds to the taps were given a bright coat of paint when the Western Region re-decorated.

A bonded warehouse with somewhat church-like windows was situated at the western end of the north platform, served by a short spur and controlled by another small ground frame. A further siding ran on behind the warehouse to form a landing further along the platform. Some photographs show a grounded coach body on the platform close to the bonded warehouse. Although there was a single slip cross-over at the end of the north platform giving access to the Down road it was not used for that purpose. Trains would run 'wrong line' to the single slip cross-overs (marked at F on the plan) before crossing.

As trains departed they would immediately cross the River Avon over a girder bridge. In later years the ends of the bridge carried the square 'Limited Clearance' warning signs, another small item not seen on many models. The tall structure of Bath station signal box was situated beyond the bridge on the south side of the line. The box was taller than usual, no doubt to aid visibility as it was sited behind a siding. (A bonus for modellers here as the box could be quickly made from two or three of the Airfix signal box kits.)

The goods yard, known officially as the Midland Bridge Road yard, covered a wide area and handled all the types of traffic one could find in any large yard of the day. The main feature of the Midland yard was the sizeable goods shed which dominated the scene. In particular, the yard dealt with considerable amounts of domestic coal, together with timber traffic.

From the Midland Bridge Road yard shunting line (shown on the track plan as the freight arrival line) access could be gained directly to the turntable in front of the Midland engine shed. Bath (Green Park) boasted two separate sheds, the S & D and the Midland, dating from the time when the two separate companies operated the services. In 1961 39 locos were allocated to the shed. Details of the actual loco allocation are shown later. Of course, at any given time a number of the engines would not be available for use for one reason or another. For example, during August 1961, 40696, 44146 and 3742 were recorded as being out of service, 53809 and 75073 were away at Derby and Eastleigh works respectively, whilst two or three Jintys were sub-shedded at Radstock.

Two roads from the 60-foot diameter turntable led directly into the Midland shed building, an attractive stone structure complementing the nearby water tower and goods shed on the south side of the line. A grounded coach body stood close by. Four tank engines could be housed comfortably within the Midland shed and the two adjacent sidings between the shed and the main line into the north platform, known as the Gas sidings, were used for stabling prepared locos. In the line's final two or three years these sidings were put to a more sombre task; to store 'dead' locomotives, with chimneys covered, which awaited their fate.

When turning a 9F 2-10-0 or West Country, great care had to be taken to position the loco accurately on the turntable otherwise wagons standing on the coal road nearby would come into collision with the loco buffers. (This is mentioned to show that modellers are not the only ones with space problems!) On summer Saturdays many locos would require turning which led to severe overcrowding of the facilities. Locos backing out of the station and needing to be turned would pull back out beyond point E on the plan before making a direct entry to the turntable road once the route had been set. At times of greatest pressure it has been known for the signalman to instruct locos coming off the station to set back well beyond point E. This was done to enable one or perhaps two prepared locos to join the same track from the Gas sidings, giving them a little extra time to set back on to a late running train waiting in the platform. Red motive power breakdown vans were usually stabled on a road alongside the coal stage road. In 1950 a breakdown crane was based at the shed.

The S & D shed had a larger holding area than the Midland shed. Chaos was increased at busy times as locos requiring both turning *and* coaling were obliged to visit *both* sheds, as the coal stage was on the S & D site. Virtually all locos required turning. Coaling, too, was necessary for most arrivals except the pilots from Templecombe shed and other engines on 'local' workings. There were four covered roads to the S & D shed with further storage and stabling lines. A water softening and sludge disposal plant was located adjacent to one of these roads. The sludge was pumped into an old tender reserved for the purpose and was periodically removed for dumping. Another regular use for this road was the stabling of the light engine which arrived from Westerleigh in the afternoon, subsequently to work the 9.15 pm freight to Birmingham. It should be mentioned, though, that this loco often went to Bristol (Barrow Road) shed and not Bath in 1960/1961. One road from the site ran down behind the shed and along by the bank of the River Avon; this was known as the 'Boat Road'. A local engineering firm was served with well wagons and a private tractor with wooden buffers was used for internal shunting.

Bath Junction, approximately half a mile from the station, was the starting point of the single line section of track at the beginning of the climb up to Combe Down tunnel. At Bath Junction signal box, situated in the angle formed by the diverging lines, trains collected or delivered the tablet which authorised the train to use the single line section to Midford. Virtually all of the engines allocated to the S & D sheds were fitted with a mechanical device for this purpose. Engines not being so fitted had to slow down and exchange the tablet by hand. The S & D yard, on the right-hand side of the Midland line to Mangotsfield, had six sidings which were used to marshal trains. There was no road access for delivery or collection of goods. Consequently there were numerous transfer workings between the S & D yard and the Midland yard. The S & D yard also gave access to the gas works which took a regular supply of coal wagons. A short siding was located near the shunting engine spur and was used by petrol tankers, their loads being discharged to the depot below on the Lower Bristol Road.

Whoops! Accidents will happen as this picture taken on November 26 1959 shows. Some empty stock being positioned in the north platform at Bath (Green Park) got out of control and went through the buffers (Peter Pike).

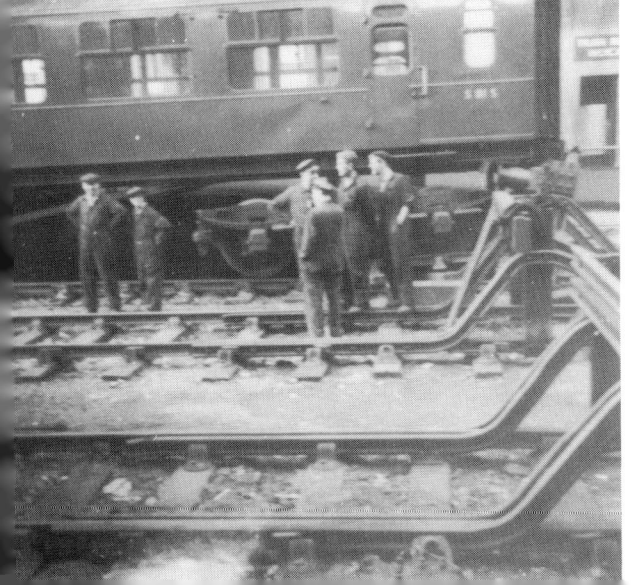

Above *Inside the S & D shed at Bath (Green Park) on June 8 1964—Jubilee 4-6-0, 45682,* Trafalgar *and Jinty 0-6-0T, 47276* (Derek Cross).

Below *Jubilee 4-6-0, 45654,* Hood, *takes coal at the S & D shed coaling stage on May 21 1958, whilst 7F 2-8-0, 53810, positions coal wagons. Notice the loaded ash wagons between the two locos* (Peter Pike).

Bath (Green Park)

Above *Bath Junction signal box, set in the angle formed by the S & D line in the foreground and the ex-Midland line to Mangotsfield. The S & D yard is in the background. Notice the tablet catching apparatus* (R. E. Toop).

Below *7F 2-8-0, 53809, stands in the water softening plant line on August 5 1962* (Roy Bullock).

Freight and other non-passenger carrying trains

In recent years the model trade has obligingly paid attention to the modeller's need for a wide variety of freight rolling stock. If a particular wagon is not produced there is probably a similar one on the market which could be adapted to suit. Parcels type vehicles are now available in a variety of shapes and sizes, an item essential when modelling the pigeon specials and perishables trains discussed later.

The track plan at Bath (Green Park) was typically Midland in character, following that company's golden rule of not using facing cross-overs unless it was totally unavoidable. Freight arrival and departure procedure was not as one might assume on first sight of the track plan. Inbound freights from the Mangotsfield direction would pass Bath Junction box and proceed down towards A as far as necessary. The train would then reverse, crossing to the Mangotsfield direction line at cross-over B, the loco coming to a stand near C. The three-way point at B would then be set for the train to pull forward into the freight arrival line up to D, where the loco was uncoupled and driven direct to the turntable. Usually a Jinty, or in later years a pannier tank, would await the train's arrival in the shunting engine spur, moving up to the brake van and then shunting as required. By virtue of the layout at Bath there were frequent transfer workings between the two yards. Freights coming off the S & D, however, would be given authority to proceed direct to the freight arrival line by a signal positioned where the line changed from single to double track. This operation did not conflict with the Midland lines in and out of the station.

Freight departures in the Mangotsfield direction were made directly from any of the roads in the Midland yard. Trains would traverse the freight arrival line and cross to the Mangotsfield line at cross-over B. S & D freights departed from the other side of the line where indicated. The train would be marshalled in one of the six roads then pulled back down the departure line to G. The train loco would then arrive and couple up near H, departure being made direct to the S & D line via the cross-over B. The headcode for freights on the S & D was one lamp below the chimney and one lamp over the right buffer.

Many of the freights would require the assistance of a banking engine. This loco would push the train up the mainly 1 in 50 curved gradient out of Bath, through Devonshire tunnel. The banker would drop off once the brake van was safely seen into the murky depths of Combe Down tunnel where the gradient changed to 1 in 100 falling. The banker would return immediately to Bath, 14 minutes being allowed for the return trip. A special 'Bath banker key' was issued by the Junction Box giving the loco authority to use the single line section and return under complete protection. During the period 1956 to 1960 4F 0-6-0, 44146, was a regular banking engine.

Freights over the S & D were mainly entrusted to the 11 7F 2-8-0s, numbered 53800-53810, which were purpose-built for the job. Almost their entire lives were spent between Bath, Evercreech Junction, Poole and Avonmouth although odd trips were taken up the Midland mainline to Derby, but that was mainly to get the loco to and from the works. The first of these locos to be withdrawn was 53800 in 1959, the last, 53807 in September 1964. 53807 worked the 11.00 am Bath to Evercreech Junction freight and returned to Bath with a brake van before having the fire dropped for the last time. The 7Fs were allocated to passenger trains on odd occasions, becoming a regular feature on certain summer Saturday expresses and local passenger services. At present there are no ready-to-run models of this class on the market, however, both N gauge and 00 gauge are represented with kits. The 00 gauge kits are available in both large and small boiler versions. No model of the S & D would be complete without one of these locos.

Other locos noted from time to time on freight services between Bath and Templecombe include the classes 4F, Stanier Black 5, BR Standard classes 4 (2-6-0/4-6-0) and 5 and, from 1961, the ex-LMS 8F 2-8-0 and ex-GW 22XX. The 3F 0-6-0 tender engines have put in odd appearances at Bath. The 7Fs, 4Fs, Jintys and pannier tanks were also employed at Bath on shunting or banking duties. Freights out of Bath to the north add Peak diesels, Crab 2-6-0s, 9F 2-10-0s, unrebuilt Patriots and, on at least two occasions, the 7F 0-8-0s to the list. 48927 (2B) was on Bath shed on January 15 1956, whilst 49230 was a visitor on January 29 1956. In April 1959, WR 2-6-0, number 5393, was based at Bath for a few days and regularly worked to Westerleigh and back. Ex-WD 90340 (36B) arrived with a freight from the north on June

11 1955, followed on January 12 1956 by sister engine, 90149 (85B). On June 29 1956 an evening freight from Bristol arrived double-headed by 8F 2-8-0 48543 and 7F 2-8-0 53804. 9F 92049 (18A) was on Bath shed on July 31 1956, and 92077 (18A) worked the 9.15 pm to Birmingham Lawley Street on May 24 1958.

The 9Fs and West Countries were not used on the Bath to Evercreech Junction freights as the turntable at Evercreech was not long enough. The West Countries were not suited to freight work anyway. In later years BR Standard class 5s were a regular feature on the 11.00 am freight out of Bath. Surprisingly enough, the Jintys were never used on freights out of Bath, although they have been noted on rare occasions around Templecombe. One interesting use for a Jinty on a model would be to represent the propelling movement which was required to get a maximum of four full coal wagons, without a brake van, to the Bath Co-op siding, about one mile up the grade towards Devonshire tunnel. This movement appears on the 1961 working timetable as being a 'when required' movement, full wagons going out at 7.25 am with empties returning at 8.10 am. The movement was more often combined with a banking job. Should the number of wagons exceed four (maximum permitted was nine) then a separate trip with a brake van at the Midford end would be required.

Freight traffic over the line was of a general nature; the main emphasis was on coal. Traffic declined gradually over the years and was accelerated after 1958 under Western control when many tons were re-routed. Even so, the 1961 working timetable still showed a reasonable amount of trains, certainly enough to keep modellers occupied in shunting. The two return workings to Midsomer Norton in that year were for coal and returning empties to and from Norton Hill Colliery. One interesting sight on freight trains would be the occasional appearance at Bath of one of Radstock's Sentinel shunters. When these locos needed to go to Barrow Road for periodic examinations the chain drive would be removed, a task nearly always performed by the same gentleman at Radstock who had discovered the 'knack' of removing these items. The free-wheeling shunter would then be marshalled into a freight train bound for Bath, coupled behind the train loco. On occasions the Sentinel would be hauled as a 'dead' engine by another loco which was going to Barrow Road for the same purpose.

A few notes of some unusual workings would be in order. During the winter months

On February 12 1955, 4F 0-6-0, 43995, ascends the first section of 1 in 50 out of Bath towards Midford (R.E. Toop).

one of Bath's Jinty locos would have its buffers removed and have snow-ploughs fitted. This loco would stand ready to go into action very swiftly, as winter in the Mendips could be extremely harsh. In the bad winter of January 1963 the Jinty was assisted by an 8F 2-8-0 when the line was engulfed for several days. Although the 8F 2-8-0s commenced regular work over the S & D in 1961, 48257 took a special freight from Bath down to Templecombe on February 29 1956. She returned light engine running tender first at least as far as Evercreech Junction. In December 1958 WD 2-8-0, 90693, was clearance tested over the line with a brake van. During the same month Western engines 2215, 3604 and 8451 were also tested, all coupled together with a brake van. 8451 failed the test at Writhlington Colliery and the class was not seen again. This was followed in January 1959 by the trial of WD 2-8-0, 90125, on the 11.00 am Bath to Evercreech Junction. As a result of this test the braking of these locos was not considered adequate and they were consequently added to the list of engines not seen on the line again. A visitor in January 1962 was WR 2-8-0, 2890, on clearance tests between Bath and Mangotsfield.

Engines which could be seen working freights in connection with the diagram for the *Pines Express* loco include West Country 4-6-2s (from 1951 to 1954), Stanier Black 5s, BR Standard 5 4-6-0s and, in later years, the 9F 2-10-0s. The engines would be turned on the Branksome triangle at the Bournemouth end of the line. The roster started with the 2.40 am Freight and Mail to Poole and Bournemouth West, known to railwaymen as the Down Mail. The freight was dropped at Poole yard with any mail vans continuing to Bournemouth West on weekdays. On Saturdays the train was for mail vans only and terminated at Poole yard. On weekdays the same loco would then bring the Up *Pines* to Bath, returning in the afternoon with the Down *Pines*, eventually to return to Bath in the early hours of the following morning at the head of the 8.10 pm Freight from Poole. This train was known to railwaymen as the Up Mail, even though mail was not carried. Incidentally, the 8.10 pm from Poole conveyed clay destined for the pottery industry of the Stoke area and on weekdays in 1961 was a continuation of a roster starting in Branksome goods yard.

The 2.40 am Down Mail carried mail in the first few vans marshalled behind the loco. Apart from those vans it was a normal freight train. One vehicle worthy of a special note was the six-wheeled brake van built especially to travel with this train, back in S & DJR days. A photograph appears in the book *Highbridge in its heyday*. It would certainly make an attractive and unusual model. Built at Highbridge Works it could be seen on the S & D up to the early 1950s, usually being confined to use on the 2.40 am and working back empty in a northbound freight. The preparation for the 2.40 am started in the late evening of the previous day when parcel vans would be positioned in the north platform at Bath (Green Park). Royal Mail vans and lorries would arrive, there being road access to this platform, whereupon the parcel vans would be loaded with the sacks of mail. The train loco then appeared, coupled up to the vans and departed at 2.40 am on the short journey to the Midland Bridge Road yard to collect the waiting freight wagons. The complete train would then set off around 2.55 am.

Two other trains involved locos working on *Pines* diagrams. The first of these was the 12.37 am parcels train from Leicester booked to arrive in Bath at 6.03 am MX on weekdays and 6.27 am on Saturdays. The arrival was normally made on the south platform. The train had made an earlier stop on its journey at Westerleigh sidings to detach vans destined for Bristol Temple Meads. This meant that on occasions the loco would arrive with as little as three vans in tow. The loco would normally be one of the more powerful breed such as the BR Standard 5, Stanier Black 5, Jubilee or the odd Royal Scot, as the return diagram for it was with the northbound *Pines Express* just after midday. Shortly after arrival the vans would be shunted. One or more vans would be held for attachment to the empty stock sitting in the carriage siding which would form the 8.15 am to Templecombe, whilst further vans would be held for attachment to the 9.03 am from Bristol Temple Meads, departing Bath at 9.53 am. Any spare vans would be shunted as needed, some going perhaps to the siding serving the loading bank behind the bonded warehouse, others going to the gas sidings adjacent to the Midland shed. These vans would sometimes go out on the 10.15 pm Perishables train to Derby.

The second train involving a *Pines* diagram was the weekdays-only 8.25 pm Perishables from Templecombe to Derby, due in Bath at 9.58 pm with departure at 10.15 pm. As a

On May 12 1952, 7F 2-8-0, 53806, in its original large boiler condition, climbs out of Bath with a south-bound freight (R.E. Toop).

perishables train, the schedule would be followed as closely as possible. Horse boxes have been noted in the formation. During the earlier part of the evening the station pilot would sort out any vans needing to be attached to the train at Bath. Departing from Bath the train was required to be in a set pattern; loco, vans for Birmingham and elsewhere, vans for Derby. This is a good excuse to get involved in a little shunting for any modellers who only have enough space to model the station area without the goods yard facilities. The outbound loco would normally be the same loco which arrived with the south-bound *Pines Express* around 3.00 pm. This means that use can be made of Royal Scots, Jubilees, Black 5s, Standard 5s, and Patriots. The odd ex-LNER B1 has been noted, such as in May 1960 when 61152 took the perishables train northbound out of Bath. A Peak can also be used if representing the last 12 to 18 months that the *Pines* ran via the S & D.

Loaded pigeon specials were a regular feature of summer Friday afternoons and Saturday mornings. These trains came from various parts of northern England with final destinations along the S & D, such as Templecombe, or sometimes even further afield to Christchurch and Weymouth. Normally the Saturday trains would arrive in the station around 6.00 am for onward transmission but occasionally later times could be encountered. Various parcels type vans were used including ex-GW Siphons. Plenty of suitable models are available from Lima, Airfix and Wrenn amongst others. The specials were usually taken over the S & D by one of the 7Fs, although motive power into Bath from the north, on the other hand, was a very mixed bag. For example, in 1958 the following locos were noted; 5934, *Kneller Hall*; 45703, *Thunderer* and a double-header in the form of Compound 41143 with Crab 42787. Other examples of double-heading were 2P 40590 and Jubilee 45655, *Keith*, and, on another occasion, WR 2-6-0s 6348 and 5330. 9Fs have also been seen. Once the pigeons had been set free during the day, the empty stock would work back to Bath in the early evening following the rush of northbound holiday expresses of the afternoon. Normal practice was for the train to return north behind the same loco or locos with which it had arrived in the morning, those engines having spent a quiet day simmering on shed.

For the modeller who wants to run other non-passenger type trains: the odd engineer's inspection saloon which travelled the line should not be forgotten. Two other examples would be Sunday ballast trains or a breakdown train going to attend a minor derailment.

Local service to Bristol Temple Meads

The pattern of services changed little in the period under discussion up to 1962, although prior to 1953 some trains ran to Bristol St Philip's. The north platform was normally used, the train loco often making use of the run round facility. In 1961 there were seven trains in each direction, the flow being towards Bristol in the morning and back to Bath in the evening. Passengers could, of course, get to and from Bristol during the rest of the day by using one of the through services. Bath managed to provide great variety even with such a small number of regular trains. The coaching stock was usually a WR B set or a Midland 2-set.

Good models suitable for this service are made by Airfix and Mainline respectively. A 1954 carriage working appendix mentioned that an empty van was worked from Bath to Bristol on the front of the 7.01 am departure. A Maunsell or Bulleid 3-set would be used on one of the morning services to get a set of coaches to Bristol to work the 9.03 am departure from there for Bournemouth West. In 00 gauge a fair representation of a Maunsell set can be made by the use of the appropriate Hornby coaches, although the Bulleid sets are only as yet available in kit form. The locals were normally worked by the Ivatt 2-6-2T engines with the BR Standard class 3 2-6-2T engines coming on the scene around 1958. Number 82041 was a regular performer on this duty.

To add variety a 3-coach set of ex-GW coaches has been seen, in red and cream livery. Ivo Peters' photographs show this set to have worked the 10.01 am departure (changed to 10.10 am by 1961) and the 6.18 pm departure. One reason for the appearance of this set of coaches and the occasional 'foreign' loco was due to the fact that Bristol (Bath Road) shed drivers had to have route knowledge should emergencies ever arise. Other steam locos noted on the local service are Ivatt 2-6-0 2MT and 4MT, pannier tanks, small prairie 2-6-2Ts (45XX), Stanier class 3 2-6-2Ts, Stanier 2P 0-4-4Ts (eg, 41903), 1P 0-4-4Ts and 2P 4-4-0s. On April 25 1955 Jinty 47275 arrived with the 11.49 am from Bristol. Examples of 2P workings are 40698 on the 7.00 pm Bristol Temple Meads to Bath (Green Park) on June 28 1954 and 40696 working the 5.40 pm Bristol Temple Meads to Bath (Green Park) on May 19 1955. Other somewhat unusual sightings were on Saturday June 5 1954 when Black 5, 44878, worked into Bath piloting 46494 on the three coach 8.10 pm from Bristol Temple Meads, and on June 23 1956 when Standard 4, 76028, took the 7.01 am out of Bath to Bristol Temple Meads.

On a model the opportunity can be taken to run one of the ex-GW railcars on this service. The 1954 summer working timetable had one rostered to arrive in Bath in the morning at 8.20 am, departing at 10.01 am, and in the evening arriving in Bath at 5.43 pm, departing at 6.18 pm. The 1957 working timetable showed only the evening trains rostered for the diesel and, by 1961, the timetable stated 'Worked by diesel SO'. Three-car diesel multiple units began to appear in place of the railcar on the evening train by early 1959. A model of these units has been produced by Lima for 00 gauge.

Even the mighty Peak diesels have had their turn at working the local. A Peak diagram was to work the 5.45 pm to Bristol arriving back at 8.50 pm. This was a fill-in duty for the loco off the southbound *Pines Express*, prior to working the 10.15 pm Perishables to Derby. It is hard to imagine another location where a Peak could be seen working with a B set. It is also possible that the odd Hymek diesel has worked the local service and records show that D1739 worked the 5.10 pm Bristol to Bath (Green Park) on June 18 1964.

On Sundays there were two trains in each direction, these being the only regular passenger service to visit the station in the winter months. Departure from Bath in the morning was at 7.55 am, arriving back at 10.30 am and the evening train departed at 7.05 pm, arriving back at 9.25 pm.

Top right *On September 24 1963 the 10.10 am local to Bristol Temple Meads waits to depart from the north platform at Bath (Green Park) behind Peak diesel number D12. BR Standard class 5, 73164, is standing in the south platform ready to depart with the 9.53 am to Bournemouth West* (Ivo Peters).

Centre right *BR Standard class 3 2-6-2T, 82041, is seen here departing from the north platform in a somewhat grimy condition with a local to Bristol Temple Meads on June 15 1965* (Derek Cross).

Right *Stanier 2-6-2T, 40174, calls at Weston (Bath) station on September 19 1953, the day on which this station was closed. The train is a Bath (Green Park) to Bristol local formed by a Midland 2-set* (R.E. Toop).

Ivatt 2-6-2T, 41243, approaches Bitton on the Midland line between Bristol Temple Meads and Bath (Green Park) on May 14 1960, at the head of Maunsell 3-set number 397 (R.E. Toop).

Through service, Bristol Temple Meads to Bournemouth West

In 1961 there were seven through trains shown in the working timetable on weekdays, four running from Bristol Temple Meads to Bournemouth West, the other three in the opposite direction. The headcode carried on the S & D was one lamp under the chimney and one lamp above the left buffer. Regular motive power for the through service between Bristol and Bath has been provided by classes Ivatt 2-6-2T, Ivatt 2-6-0 2MT and 4MT, and Stanier class 3 2-6-2T, in particular 40116. On occasions Stanier Black 5s and 2P 4-4-0s have been seen. For example, 2P 40568 was seen heading the 3.40 pm Bournemouth West to Bristol Temple Meads (7.03 pm off Bath (Green Park)), tender first, on August 8 1956. Another tender first working was with BR Standard class 5, 73051, on the 9.03 am from Bristol Temple Meads on September 7 1955. Un-rebuilt Patriot 45509 (17A) made an appearance on July 15 1955 with the 4.21 pm arrival in Bath. The Saturday 8.20 am and 9.03 am from Bristol were sometimes used to get locos to Bath to power later northbound trains. (The 8.20 am had been deleted by 1961 and so is not shown in the timetable in the appendices.)

Motive power for the through service on the S & D itself over the period has been drawn from classes 2P, West Country, 4F, Stanier Black 5, Ivatt 2-6-0 4MT, BR Standard 5, BR Standard 4 (4-6-0 and 2-6-0), BR Standard 4 2-6-4T and 9F. Platform usage could vary depending on circumstances but to give examples the 4.21 pm and 7.05 pm departures to Bournemouth West used the north platform whilst the 4.30 pm and 7.03 pm to Bristol used the south. The loco to continue the journey north or south would normally come off shed a few minutes before the arrival of the incoming train and stand in wait at E on the plan. Once the train had arrived in the alloted platform the new loco would set back and couple.

In true S & D style, stock and motive power varied widely over the period. In the early 1950s ex-LSWR 3-sets were in use, set numbers 421 and 348 being examples. These old coaches were gradually replaced by Southern Region green Maunsell 3-sets in the series 390-399. A strengthening coach was normally added to these sets during the summer service. On occasions this would be a red and cream Midland Region coach when, because of design differences, the corridor connection would not be made. From time to time during the summer the running authorities would commandeer the Maunsell sets for use elsewhere, replacing them with the original ex-LSWR sets.

In 1950 the main sources of motive power were the Ivatt 2-6-0 4MTs, the Stanier Black 5s and various members of the 4F 0-6-0 and 2P 4-4-0 classes. In March 1951 the Southern Region arranged tests to find a suitable replacement loco for the Stanier Black 5s, as the London Midland Region were requesting their return. For convenience, the S & D portion of the through service was used for the testing.

These tests added another class of loco to the already varied scene on the S & D in the shape of the recently built Battle of Britain class pacific, number 34109, *Sir Trafford Leigh Mallory*. Incidentally, the driver on the first day of the tests on the 11.40 am from Bournemouth West as far as Bath was Donald Beale, one of the line's best known 'characters', whose exploits behind the regulator have been recounted in Peter Smith's two captivating books about the line, written from the driver's view point. The tests were completed favourably as far as the through services were concerned, although the class needed a pilot over the Mendips when handling the *Pines Express* or the holiday expresses with over eight coaches in tow. Three West Country class locos were subsequently allocated to Bath where they were to remain shedded until 1954. The locos concerned were 34040/41/42. Bournemouth Central always supplied 34043/44 to cover when required. The West Country class were rostered as necessary which even gives the modeller licence to use one on Bath Station carriage shunting duties in the early evening. There were two unusual occurrences on this service in 1953 when, firstly a Southern Region Q class 0-6-0 worked up to Bath from Poole on the 9.28 pm (later 8.10 pm) goods train returning with the 9.53 am off Bath and secondly, a Carlisle-based Black 5 worked over the line in June, fitted with a small snow-plough.

In 1954 the authorities once again considered that tests were needed to find a suitable alternative to the Southern Region West Country class, which was prone to be a trifle light-footed at times. In the first two weeks of March of that year the 11.40 am from Bournemouth West and 4.26 pm back (4.21 pm in 1961) was hauled by U 2-6-0, 31621, and U1 2-6-0, 31906. These tests were not successful so the locos were not seen again apart from very rare fill-in duties (covering for failed locos). One such trip was on July 28 1961 when 31628 was in charge of the 1.10 pm from Bournemouth West, returning on the 7.05 pm from Bath. The S & D received BR Standard class 5 numbers 73051/2 in May 1954, followed in June by 73050. The late arrival of 73050 was due to its involvement with the International Railway Congress Exhibition held at Willesden during the last week of May. (Photographs of the event appear on page 549 of the August 1954 issue of *Railway Magazine*.) This loco arrived in Bath in immaculate condition having been specially prepared for the exhibition.

The attachment and detachment of parcel vans was a feature of the through service. The 1954 carriage working appendix noted that a van was rostered to arrive in Bath attached to the rear of the 9.05 am from Bristol Temple Meads (9.03 am in 1961). Another van, or vans, would be attached to this before departure, having come off the Leicester parcels train earlier in the morning. Other van workings noted were an empty van on the rear of the 6.40 pm from Bournemouth West (6.48 pm in 1961) and a van on the rear of the 12.55 pm from Bournemouth West (1.10 pm in 1961) on Saturdays only.

Close on the heels of the BR Standard class 5 came the BR Standard class 4 2-6-0 in 1955. The class were used regularly on the service following the trial of 76012 in March of that year, and became almost exclusive motive power for the roster which started with the 6.40 pm from Bournemouth West (6.48 pm in 1961) and continued next day with the 6.55 am Down from Bath (6.48 am in 1961), the 12.55 pm Up from Bournemouth West (1.10 pm in 1961), finishing with the 7.05 pm Down from Bath in the evening.

Class T9 4-4-0s appeared several times on the 3.40 pm Up, covering for failures of the Standard class 4s. Every effort was made to run this train from Bournemouth West on schedule as it conveyed a van at the rear, transporting mail. At Bath a loco would attach any further vans to the train, or mail bags would be loaded in the guard's compartment. This train would then depart at 7.03 pm to make connection with the 7.25 pm Bristol to Newcastle mail train at Mangotsfield.

Up to 1956 the 11.40 am from Bournemouth West ran through to Gloucester from Bristol on Mondays to Thursdays, being extended to Derby on Fridays only. In 1957 the train ran only as far as Bristol Temple Meads except on

Fridays. On that day the train was usually composed of eight coaches. Arrival at Bath was at 1.50 pm whereupon a loco would couple to the rear five coaches and depart for Derby at 1.55 pm. Another loco would then couple on to the remaining three coaches and depart to Bristol Temple Meads at the usual time of 2.05 pm.

As mentioned before, the rolling stock for the service was usually a Maunsell 3-set but this did not preclude the use of the occasional set of WR stock with coaches of Hawksworth and Collett design being seen. The 5.58 am Bristol Temple Meads to Bournemouth West and 1.10 pm return were regularly WR stock. If the modeller has chosen the period 1957 to 1959 then a good variation in coaching stock colour schemes is possible. It was in 1956 that the management of British Railways declared that the red and cream livery was to be phased out, being replaced by a standard lined maroon. Southern Region was to keep its green livery and certain Western Region expresses would re-appear in chocolate and cream. So, in the period around 1958 mixed liveries were part of the scene and help to create an interesting spectacle on a model. To give an example during this period, Maunsell set 393 was in red and cream, set 399 was in green, and set 396 had red and cream brake ends with a green composite in the middle. One way of 'doubling' the passenger stock on a model railway is to paint each side of the vehicles in a different livery to suit the period being modelled. This idea will normally only be applied to stock which is only viewed from one side, ie, no reverse loops, etc.

In 1958 the Midland Region requested the return of the two remaining Stanier Black 5s shedded at Bath, numbers 44917 and 45440. Their places were taken by Standard 5s, 73019 and 73028. During the winter service of 1959/60, Bulleid sets in the series 963-972 appeared. One of the most significant dates on the S & D calendar was on March 29 1960. A 9F 2-10-0, number 92204, was tested in both directions over the line with a 350-ton train in very bad weather conditions. The success of these trials led to the allocation of 92203/04/05 and 06 to Bath shed during June 1960 for the duration of the summer service. Primarily, the 9Fs were in Bath to haul the holiday expresses but they were put to good use on the through service at other times during the week. Even 92220, *Evening Star*, spent at least part of the summers of 1962 and 1963 hauling these trains. By 1961 a 3-set of Midland Region corridor stock with odd strengthening coaches could be seen along with the Bulleid sets. Decline had set in and by 1964 coaching stock was a very mixed bag of Southern, Western and Midland Region styles, including BR Mark 1 coaches.

Although the service normally only employed three or four coaches this number could be greatly exceeded on summer Saturdays or on days preceding and following Bank Holidays. On summer Saturdays the 6.48 am and 9.53 am were invariably double-headed out of Bath, in order to get pilot engines down to Evercreech Junction for northbound expresses later in the morning. Double-heading occurred at other times on this service to save a path being used up by a light engine on busy days. To add final variety to the motive power used on the through service over the S & D the 8F 2-8-0 can be added from around 1963. The BR 2-6-4T locos entered service in November of that year. Working the train between Bath and Bristol, Hymek diesels (D70XX series) and, on summer Saturdays, Patriot steam locos have also been seen in the 1960s.

One of many interesting examples of how the S & D staff tried to do their best for their passengers occurred on Saturday, November 21 1959. An evening local from Bristol Temple Meads arrived in Bath conveying seven passengers off the 85-minute-late 12.48 pm from York. These passengers needed to go to Bournemouth but, because of the late running of the York train, they had missed the 6.08 pm SO Bristol to Bournemouth West through train. The railway staff laid on a one-coach-special hauled by an 0-6-0 engine which ran non-stop from Bath to Templecombe to make a connection.

On Sundays regular passenger trains only ran over the S & D during the summer service. The service in 1961 was:
Dep 9.30 am to Bournemouth West, arriving back at 9.27 pm
Arr 10.01 from Bristol Temple Meads
Dep 10.06 am to Bournemouth West
Arr 12.02 pm from Bournemouth West
Dep 12.07 pm to Bristol Temple Meads
Arr 7.42 pm from Bristol Temple Meads
Dep 7.47 pm to Bournemouth West
Arr 9.45 pm from Bournemouth West
Dep 9.50 pm to Bristol Temple Meads.

In 1959 the 12.02 pm arrival from Bournemouth West and returning 7.47 pm departure were rostered for a West Country, changing in 1960 to a Standard 5.

Bath (Green Park)

Above Bath (Green Park) on April 10 1954. Class 2P 4-4-0, 40697, departs from the north platform with the 3.30 pm Bristol Temple Meads to Bournemouth West through train, Maunsell 3-set 396. In the carriage siding sister-engine, 40509, waits with the stock which will form the 4.37 pm to Templecombe. Notice the cattle wagon. In the south platform Ivatt 2-6-2T, 41240, waits to take the 12.55 pm Up from Bournemouth West on the final leg of its journey to Bristol Temple Meads (Ivo Peters).

Below Ivatt 2-6-2T, 41208, leaves the south platform at 7.03 pm on April 26 1958 with the 3.40 pm from Bournemouth West. In the north platform, making a rare appearance in Bath, is T9 4-4-0, 30706, about to depart to Bournemouth West at 7.05 pm. Notice the water taps between the tracks and the empty stock in the carriage siding (R.E. Toop).

Above BR Standard class 5, 73054, waits (at point E on the Bath track diagram) for Ivatt 2-6-2T, 41304, to arrive with a Bristol to Bournemouth West through train on July 18 1963 (Derek Cross).

Below A little later, the same train (73054) is seen passing the S & D shed on its way up to Bath Junction. The sludge tender can be seen on the left of the picture. It bears the wording To be returned to water softening plant Bath (Derek Cross).

Local service to Templecombe

The 1961 weekday working timetable showed five departures from Bath to Templecombe but only three in the other direction from Templecombe to Bath. Under this heading the inbalance has been put right by including two other trains terminating at Bath. The first is the 10.46 am arrival from Broadstone, the second being the 10.21 pm arrival from Bournemouth West. They have been included as the stock formed Templecombe trains on a rotating basis, and both trains spent 30 minutes and 40 minutes respectively at Templecombe on their journey up to Bath. The coaching stock normally used on this service was a 3-set with the occasional strengthening coach, much the same as the through service between Bristol Temple Meads and Bournemouth West.

In the 1950s the Templecombe locals were, in the main, the province of the 2P 4-4-0s and the 4F 0-6-0s. In 1956 the BR Standard class 4 4-6-0s started to play a regular role, 75071/72/73 being the first allocated to the S & D. Templecombe shed's first member of the class was 75027 in 1960, followed later by 75002/04/07/09 and 23. In 1960 the Collett 22XX class appeared. One of the earliest workings of a 22XX was on December 19 1960 when class member 3216 worked the 12 noon Templecombe to Bath and 4.15 pm return. Sister class members, 3210 and 3215, for example, have been noted on these trains, in fact 3215 was fitted with a tablet catcher. In November of 1963 the BR Standard class 4 2-6-4T locos started work on the S & D, the Templecombe locals being one of their duties. The 7F 2-8-0s have often been rostered on these workings, particularly on Saturdays during the summer. It is also likely that the 8F 2-8-0s have been used, possibly in the line's last few months of life.

As far as Templecombe trains were concerned the day started shortly after the arrival of the Leicester parcels train. Anything up to three vans were detached from that train for later attachment to the stock waiting in the carriage siding. Departure of the first service, the 8.15 am, would normally be from the south platform, the north platform having been occupied by a Bristol Temple Meads local which departed a few minutes earlier. On very rare occasions it has been known for drivers of the 8.15 am to call for a pilot loco when the load has been considered too much for one engine alone. At 8.42 am Bath saw the arrival of the first passenger train of the day off the S & D, the 7.00 am from Templecombe. This train would normally arrive in the south platform, as the north platform would be holding the 8.22 am arrival from Bristol Temple Meads waiting to form the 10.10 am departure back. The 8.42 am arrival was generally a 3-set with a Midland 2-set coupled next to the loco. Once the passengers had disembarked, the stock would be shunted into the carriage siding adjacent to the south platform, and the Midland 2-set uncoupled from the 3-set. The stock remained unused until around 4.20 pm when the 3-set would be required to form the 4.37 pm departure to Templecombe from where it would form the 7.00 am back the next day. The Midland 2-set remained in the carriage siding until around 6.00 pm when it would be required to form the 6.05 pm to Binegar, arriving back in Bath at 8.03 pm. (The Binegar train is detailed in the next section.)

Various odd wagons were attached to the Templecombe service as and when required. Small, open wagons were noted occasionally, for example taking urgent spares down to Templecombe loco shed, usually on the 3.20 pm. The 1.10 pm from Bath to Templecombe was the first choice of the authorities when sending loaded cattle wagons down to the cattle merchant in Wincanton, although the 3.20 pm and 4.37 pm have been used for this traffic. Normally only one cattle wagon would be seen, but two have been observed on rare occasions when business was brisk for the merchant. Box vans were attached to the trains at various locations if the traffic was sufficiently urgent. A photograph in the Midsomer Norton chapter shows this manoeuvre about to be performed.

The 7.33 am from Broadstone, which had earlier spent half an hour in Templecombe Upper, was the next train to arrive under this heading, at 10.46 am in the north platform. It would then be shunted to the run-round road adjacent to the north platform and later form the 1.10 pm back to Templecombe. 1.35 pm was the next arrival, the stock probably remaining in the north platform to form the 3.20 pm departure. Incidentally, around 4.15 pm was a busy time in the station, as a look at the timetable will show; three trains with five locos. Stock off the 6.00 pm arrival in the north platform would be shunted to the carriage siding, where it would remain to form the 8.15 am departure next morning.

Background photograph BR Standard class 4 4-6-0, 75007, swings left at Bath Junction on July 18 1963 with a Bath to Templecombe local of three Bulleid coaches and a six-wheeled van. The track to the right of the train is the shunting line (Derek Cross).

Inset right 7F 2-8-0, 53807, and 4F 0-6-0, 44558, prepare to leave Bath (Green Park) on a damp June 6 1964 with the 8.15 am to Templecombe. The need for double-heading the 8.15 am ceased in 1962, but the train had two locos on this occasion as they were required to work a special from Bournemouth over the S & D the next day (Derek Cross).

Inset below right A cold scene at Bath (Green Park) on March 5 1966. 8F 2-8-0, 48706, brings empty Bulleid stock out of the carriage siding. The bonded warehouse is on the left of the picture (Derek Cross).

Local service to Binegar

In some ways this train, running down to Binegar and back in the early evening on Monday to Friday as it did, was the odd man out of the line's services. No evidence has come to light to show that the rolling stock was ever anything else but a Midland 2-set which arrived in Bath on the 7.00 am from Templecombe. Once the local from Bristol Temple Meads had arrived in the south platform at 5.44 pm, very often formed by the ex-GW railcar as mentioned earlier, the train loco for the 6.05 pm to Binegar would collect its empty stock from the carriage siding. It would then reverse into the south platform, taking care not to collide with the train already occupying the buffer stop end. At 6.05 pm, with the usual Ivatt 2-6-2T or Standard class 3 2-6-2T at the head, the train would depart, leaving the south platform clear once again for the Bristol Temple Meads local to depart at 6.18 pm. The train loco ran round at Binegar and left at 7.10 pm, arriving back in Bath at 8.03 pm, the stock being used later as described in the preceding section. Regular locos on this service in the 1950s were 41241/42/43 and in the early 1960s, 82041. Other motive power has been provided by a 2P 4-4-0 on at least one occasion, namely August 24 1955. On April 15 1957 the two coaches had Standard 5, 73049, at the head. A Jinty was used at times when the bottom of the barrel had to be scraped to find motive power. 1P 0-4-4T, number 58072, was borrowed from Highbridge shed during a temporary shortage of tank locos at Bath during late April and early May 1955 and worked the service regularly for that short period.

Under the overall roof at Bath (Green Park) on May 27 1958. The front train with an Ivatt 2-6-2T at the head is the 6.05 pm for Binegar, whilst the train behind is the 6.18 pm departure for Bristol Temple Meads headed by 0-6-0PT, 3676 (R.E. Toop).

Bath (Green Park)

The *Pines Express*

The *Pines Express* was the principal train to run over the S & D line on Monday to Friday, with slightly altered timings applied on summer Saturdays. The express takes it name from the countryside at the Bournemouth end of the journey where pine trees abound. The train connected Bournemouth and Manchester via the S & D with a restaurant car service until it was re-routed in 1962. On weekdays in 1961 the Up *Pines* left Bournemouth West at 9.45 am and called at Poole, Blandford Forum, Stalbridge, Evercreech Junction (where a pilot would usually be attached) and Shepton Mallet, with arrival in Bath (Green Park) at 11.56 am. Departure from Bath in the northbound direction was at 12.01 pm to serve various intermediate stations to Manchester and Liverpool Lime Street with through coaches to Sheffield. The Down *Pines* arrived in Bath from the Manchester direction at 3.03 pm. Timings at Bath varied slightly from 1950 to 1961 but were always around the 3.00 pm mark. First stop was Evercreech Junction, where the pilot would be detached, followed by Blandford Forum, Broadstone and Poole with final arrival in Bournemouth West at 5.32 pm. This train would always use the south platform at Bath. When things were running smoothly the loco for both the Up and Down *Pines* would be that which took the 2.40 am Freight and Mail down the line earlier in the day.

Although the loco on the Down Mail was booked for the returning *Pines Express*, failures did, of course, occur from time to time. Failures with Standard 5s were comparatively rare. If, in the mid-1950s, for example, the loco hauling the Down Mail portion of the diagram was to fail it would invariably be replaced by a 4F, which would work the train to Bournemouth West. If Bournemouth Central shed could not (or would not!) send out a West Country as a replacement, then Templecombe shed would despatch a 2P light engine to Branksome. The 2P would then assist the 4F back up to Bath with the Up *Pines*, where, hopefully, a suitable replacement would be found to work the Down *Pines*. If one was not available the two engines would take the *Pines* down to Bournemouth West and the 4F would return in the evening on the final freight part of the diagram from Poole. By 1961, that diagram started as the 7.35 pm from Branksome goods yard, followed by the 8.10 pm from Poole.

Normally the coaching stock of the *Pines Express* would be of a regular smart appearance made up of the latest available coaches, 12 in number being the usual load during the summer or at Bank Holiday periods. At other times 10 or 11 coaches were more usual. In the early 1950s these were ex-LMS types in red and cream livery, which changed gradually over the years to maroon. BR Mark 1 coaches were regular in the train's final years over the S & D. On summer Saturdays the express was sometimes not its orderly set of coaching stock. In fact, the last Up *Pines Express* on Saturday, September 8 1962 conveyed an ex-LNER Gresley coach and one Mark 1 coach in chocolate and cream livery. The restaurant car was an ex-LMS 12-wheeled vehicle almost daily until around 1961.

On Mondays and Fridays during the summer service of the 1950s the *Pines* was supplemented by a train to and from Sheffield. On those days, the *Pines* did not convey the Sheffield portion. This train had been deleted prior to the 1961 timetable shown in the appendices but, nevertheless, ran on many occasions. In 1957, for example, the train left Bournemouth West at 9.30 am, making the same calls as the *Pines* with the exception of Shepton Mallet and arrived in Bath at 11.45 am with departure to Sheffield at 11.49 am. The *Pines* would be hard on its heels, arriving only a few minutes later. In the opposite direction the train left Sheffield Midland at 10.10 am to arrive in Bath at 2.48 pm. Departure from Bath was at 2.53 pm, making the same stops as the *Pines* which would again be chasing down shortly behind. Arrival in Bournemouth West was at 5.13 pm. A regular loco for this duty was a West Country.

In the 1957 timetable, a Q train was booked to depart Bournemouth West at 9.55 am on weekdays. This train was run on occasions such as the Thursday prior to and the Tuesday after a Bank Holiday weekend, when traffic would be heavy. When the train ran, the preceding 9.45 am would be formed of Sheffield-only coaches, normally eight in number, and the 9.55 am would, in fact, be the *Pines* stock and go to Manchester/Liverpool.

Motive power on the *Pines* in 1950 was a regular Black 5 duty with a 2P 4-4-0 as pilot over the Mendips in each direction as and when required. Between 1951 and 1954 the Black 5s played a supporting role to the West

Country pacifics which had been allocated to Bath following the 1951 trials with the Bristol to Bournemouth West through service. As mentioned earlier the 'light pacifics' were somewhat too 'light' for the *Pines* duty and the freight part of the diagram. As a consequence, in 1954, the newly arrived BR Standard class 5 locos were given the duty, although on summer Saturdays the train was rostered for a West Country with a 2P pilot from Evercreech Junction. The *Pines* pilot was invariably the 2P to have most recently returned from overhaul at Derby works or at least a loco in very good condition. Bath's remaining Black 5s handled the express at odd times over the period before 1958 when they were returned to the Midland Region.

34039, *Boscastle*, was the first rebuilt West Country to travel over the line when it headed the Up *Pines* relief on June 19 1959. In the summer of 1960 the 9F 2-10-0s made their debut on the *Pines* and what a splendid sight it was. 1961 was the last year in which the 2Ps acted as pilots, being replaced in September by the Standard class 4 4-6-0s. Possibly the last Black 5 working on the Down *Pines* was on May 25 1962 when 44945 was in charge. The 9Fs were not usually used on Friday trains. They would normally spend the day on shed to minimise the risk of failure, which would cause problems the next day.

In 1962, the express was re-routed as part of the Western Region's general run down of services over the S & D. The new route took the train via Oxford, Basingstoke and Southampton. The last Up and Down *Pines* were worked by 92220, *Evening Star*, which had earlier been specially transferred to Bath shed. In particular, the last Up *Pines* (on Saturday, September 8 1962) is worthy of special mention. Donald Beale, spoken of earlier, relinquished the driving seat on this auspicious occasion to his fireman, Peter Smith (who was passed for driving duties), to be assisted by fireman Aubrey Punter. Smith gives a detailed account of this exchange of duties and the final northbound run in his book, *Mendips Engineman*, and how it set up a record for being the heaviest train ever to be hauled over the Mendips by a single engine.

Departing or arriving from the north at Bath the train was usually hauled by a Stanier Black 5 or a BR Standard class 5. 2P 4-4-0s have occasionally acted as pilots. In the final two or three years Jubilees, Patriots and Royal Scots were noted on the duty. In March 1961 Britannia 70014, *Iron Duke*, arrived with the southbound *Pines*. Another milestone in the story of the *Pines Express* is the commencement of the winter timetable for 1961 when Peak diesels became a regular source of motive power. Other notable occurrences in and out of Bath include the sighting of two Midland Compounds heading north and the use of ex-LNER B1s. In May 1960, B1 61152 arrived with the southbound *Pines* and returned north with the 10.15 pm Perishables. Later in the same month 61027 arrived with the southbound *Pines*, stayed on shed until next day and then worked the northbound train. In August 1960, 61176 was seen. June 10 1961 saw 46100, *Royal Scot*, depart northbound.

Below left *The north-bound* Pines Express *arrives from Bournemouth West on July 3 1954 behind 2P 4-4-0, 40563, and BR Standard class 5, 73050* (Ivo Peters).
Above *The Down* Pines Express *leaves Bath (Green Park) on May 18 1959 behind West Country 4-6-2, 34044,* Woolacombe, *piloted by BR Standard class 5, 73028* (R.E. Toop).
Below *Now preserved BR Standard class 5, 73050, pilots sister-engine 73052 into Bath on April 20 1957 with the Up* Pines Express *from Bournemouth West. The first vehicle is the 12-wheeled dining car* (R.E. Toop).

Summer Saturdays

Bath (Green Park) can be called the northern gateway to the S & D. The attraction of the station to the modeller and the enthusiast must surely be the vast range of motive power and rolling stock which was used on a daily basis, but which swelled out of all proportion on these infamous summer Saturdays. Locos from such diverse sheds as St Rollox, Preston and Nine Elms have been seen to name but three. Another location in this country offering the same sights as Bath (Green Park) would be very difficult to find. Possibly Oxford would be a major contender but there again it is doubtful that a reduction in size and scope for model purposes would be acceptable. Take into account that in the summer of 1961, Bath (Green Park) handled well over 50 passenger trains plus pigeon specials and a parcels train on a Saturday, all having to use one of only two platforms. One interesting shunting manoeuvre was the use of the gas tanker, normally stabled on the carriage siding, filling the tanks of needy restaurant cars. The benefits to a modeller of representing a summer Saturday are many with coaching stock of all types being seen over the period. These include ex-LNER Gresley articulated stock, for example, and, on July 26 1952, an ex-GC Barnum brake end saloon on the 7.43 am Birmingham to Bournemouth West. As the days of the week passed by and another Saturday loomed closer, the shed staff at Bath would 'kidnap' incoming foreign locomotives for possible use, not returning them to their home depots until after the weekend.

Up to and including the summer of 1960 the holiday expresses were given a three digit reporting number before being replaced in 1961 by the four character headcode system. A note of warning when looking at photographs. Just because a loco shows a particular headcode it does not necessarily follow that the train behind it is in fact that same train! At busy times it has been known for staff to forget to amend the headcode before working a subsequent train. Wherever possible all the photographs in this book have had their accuracy verified from at least one source or another.

A transcription of the Saturday timetable as at midsummer 1961 can be found in the appendices. It is extremely unlikely that the timetable on summer Saturdays was ever adhered to exactly, because of distances travelled by many trains and the inevitable bottleneck of the single line section between Bath and Midford. Therefore the platform indications on the timetable should not be

Jubilee 45626, Seychelles, leaves Bath on August 12 1961 with the 11.12 am Bournemouth West to Sheffield, whilst Stanier Black 5, 45447, waits to enter the vacated platform with the Cleethorpes to Exmouth train (Malcolm Lewis).

treated as being regular. By way of comparison to 1961, there were 13 scheduled Down holiday expresses in 1954, with 11 in the reverse direction. These were supplemented on Saturday July 31, for example, by relief trains from Kidsgrove, Tunstall, Stoke and Loughborough, all arriving and departing from Bath before 4.00 am. A further relief from Leicester followed down in the early afternoon. In the northbound direction reliefs were run to Manchester, Birmingham/Coventry and Bournville/Walsall.

Should the modeller wish to split the difference and choose 1957 as his period then there are four additional trains which can be slotted into the schedules shown for 1961. As was usual over the years, odd minutes were added or deleted to the timings, but this did not materially effect the sequence of events on Saturdays. The trains concerned are two Bristol Temple Meads to Bournemouth West through trains and two holiday expresses. The 8.20 am Bristol Temple Meads to Bournemouth West arrived in Bath at 9.00 am and departed at 9.05 am. A corresponding return train left Bournemouth West at 2.45 pm arriving in Bath at 5.11 pm, departing in the Bristol direction at 5.28 pm. The first of the holiday expresses was the 11.00 pm FO Derby to Bournemouth West arriving in Bath at 2.40 am departing at 2.45 am. The second was the 10.30 am Liverpool to Bournemouth West arriving in Bath at 3.52 pm, departing five minutes later at 3.57 pm. Four other holiday expresses arrived and departed in existing timings but had their destinations altered. Another slight alteration was that in 1957 a return train ran from Cleethorpes to Bournemouth West but, by 1961, had been re-routed to become the return Cleethorpes to Exmouth train via Templecombe. The stock of this train often contained Gresley coaches. It was also somewhat unusual in that the majority of coaches were Southern Region green liveried vehicles.

The following table shows the typical rostered locos and pilots which were used between Bath and Evercreech Junction (or Templecombe) during the summer of 1961. It should be noted, though, that over the years northbound expresses sometimes had pilots detached at Binegar and the pilot off the 9.53 am from Bath was usually detached at Shepton Mallet.

Down trains

	Reporting number	Pilot	Train loco
7.43 am Birmingham—B West	1 O 88	—	Std 5
9.08 am Birmingham—B West	1 O 90	2P	Std 5
7.35 am Nottingham—B West	1 O 91	—	9F
7.00 am Cleethorpes—Exmouth	1 O 92	2P	4F
9.35 am Sheffield—B West	1 O 93	—	9F
7.43 am Bradford—B West	1 O 94	—	9F
10.30 am Manchester—B West	1 O 95	2P	W Country
10.55 am Manchester—B West	1 O 97	Std 4 4-6-0	W Country
9.53 am Bath—B West	2 B 92	2P	Std 5
4.37 pm Bath—Templecombe	2 B 92	—	Std 4 4-6-0

Up trains

	Reporting number	Pilot	Train loco
8.40 am B West—Bradford	1 N 46	—	9F
9.25 am B West—Manchester	1 M 02	2P	W Country
9.45 am B West—Manchester	1 M 04	2P	9F
9.55 am B West—Leeds	1 N 66	—	9F
10.05 am B West—Derby	1 M 06	Std 4 4-6-0	Std 5
10.32 am B West—Manchester	1 M 07	2P	W Country
11.12 am B West—Sheffield	1 E 58	2P	7F
12.20 pm B West—Nottingham	1 M 08	2P	W Country
10.42 am Exmouth—Cleethorpes	1 E 59	—	7F
1.10 pm B West—Bristol T M	2 B 93	—	Std 4 2-6-0

Locos at Bath (Green Park) shed (code 82F) on Saturday, August 12 1961

Home based locos available
40697 40700
41242/43
44558/59/61
47275 47316 47465/96 47557
53803/04/06/07/08/10
73047/50/51/52/54/87
75071/72
82004/41
92000/01/06 92212
7790

Home based locos not available
40696   44146   53809
73019   75073   3742

Visiting locos
40564 82G   40569 82G   40634 82G
44422 82G
44742 6G   44745 27A   44857 55A   44859 21A
44920 21A   44963 21A   44964 9E   45238 14A
45447 21A
45626 17A   45690 82E   45726 5A
46103 21A
48507 18A
73155 41C
75027 82G
76027 71A
92136 21A
34041 71B   34043 71B   34045 71B
3210 82G

Daytime through trains at Bath (Green Park) on Saturday, August 12 1961

Train from		Pilot	Loco	Train to	Pilot	Loco	Load
7.43 am	Birmingham	—	73087	Bournemouth West	—	73051	8
8.16 am	Bournemouth West	—	?	Loughborough	—	44963	8 ECS
8.40 am	Bournemouth West	—	92001	Bradford	—	44753	11
9.08 am	Birmingham	—	44920	Bournemouth West	40700	73052	10
9.25 am	Bournemouth West	40569	34045	Liv/Manchester	—	73087	12
9.45 am	Up Pines Express	40634	92006	Manchester	—	46103	11
7.35 am	Nottingham	—	44918	Bournemouth West	—	53807	10
9.55 am	Bournemouth West	—	92000	Leeds	—	44859	8
10.05 am	Bournemouth West	75027	73054	Derby	—	45238	11
10.32 am	Bournemouth West	40697	34043	Manchester	—	44964	8
11.12 am	Bournemouth West	40564	53810	Sheffield	—	45626	10
7.00 am	Cleethorpes	—	45447	Exmouth	40569	44422	8
10.40 am	Exmouth	3210	53806	Cleethorpes	—	44920	11
9.35 am	Sheffield	—	44857	Bournemouth West	—	92001	10
7.43 am	Bradford	—	45690	Bournemouth West	—	92006	10
12.00 pm	Bournemouth West	—	73050	Kidsgrove	—	44742	8
12.20 pm	Bournemouth West	40700	34041	Nottingham	—	44918	10
10.30 am	Down Pines Express	—	92136	Bournemouth West	40564	34045	12
10.55 am	Manchester	—	73155	Bournemouth West	75027	34041	12

The 12.00 noon relief from Bournemouth West often ran even though the working timetable did not show it. On August 12 1961 it ran to Kidsgrove, whereas on August 19 it ran to Huddersfield. Two pigeon specials came into Bath on August 12, although their ultimate destinations are unknown. The 1.10 am from Crewe came in behind 45726 5A and the 1.00 am from Preston behind 44745 27A.

A further note about the use of B1s. In June 1959, 61164 arrived with the 9.08 am from Birmingham and in June 1960, 61167 took the 11.12 am Bournemouth West to Sheffield northbound out of Bath.

Top right *A typical summer Saturday scene for the 8.15 am departure to Templecombe from the south platform with the train being double-headed. In this instance the pilot is 4F 0-6-0, 44560. In the north platform Ivatt 2-6-2T, 41243, waits to depart with the 8.11 am local to Bristol Temple Meads* (Derek Cross).

Centre right *The north-bound* Pines Express *leaves Bath on August 12 1961 behind Royal Scot, 46103,* Royal Scots Fusilier (Malcolm Lewis).

Right *Stanier Black 5, 44920, leaves Bath on August 12 1961 with the Exmouth to Cleethorpes train passing 2P 4-4-0, 40564, and Stanier Black 5, 44918* (Malcolm Lewis).

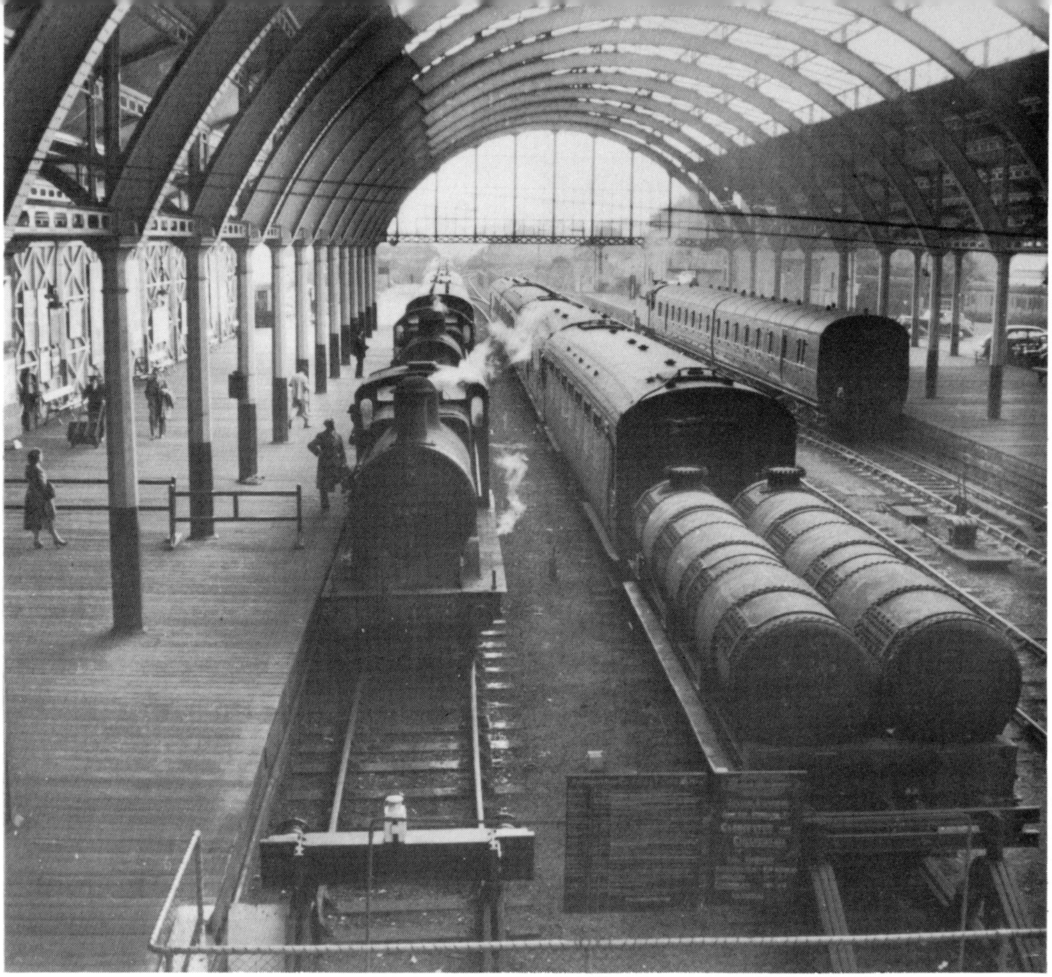

Above *Looking outwards from the buffer stops at Bath (Green Park) on September 11 1954. 3F 0-6-0, 43441, and 7F 2-8-0, 53805, have arrived in the south platform with an express from Bournemouth West. In the carriage siding is the stock from the 7.00 am from Templecombe together with the gas tanker. In the north platform Ivatt 2-6-2T, 41241, prepares to leave with a B set for Bristol Temple Meads. Notice the overall roof, the wooden platforms, the north platform ground frame and the neatly chalked information boards* (Ivo Peters).

Below *Bath (Green Park) on July 20 1957, looking from a train on the south platform out towards Bath station signal box. A north-bound express has just departed from the north platform leaving the road free for Stanier Black 5, 44808, and BR Standard class 5, 73050, to back out for disposal on shed* (R.E. Toop).

Special trains

Over the years various 'specials' went over the S & D, either as part of a more varied itinerary or as S & D excursions in their own right. Under this heading the liberty has been taken to include a somewhat unusual event in 1953. This concerns one week in April of that year when Bath's turntable went out of action. Use was made of the triangle at Mangotsfield, which meant that as many as five locos would be seen coupled together on their journey up the line. It is suggested that the modeller does not try to recreate this scene as it is possible that damage may be caused to motors and controllers. The effect can be achieved just as well by two locos coupled together. In fact it is a good idea when having an operating session to 'throw a spanner in the works' occasionally, eg, make a turntable unavailable. The turntable at Bath was again out of action for about a week during April 1960.

A notable special was on Sunday, April 25 1954 when a School class 4-4-0 30932, *Blundells*, made an appearance on the line. It arrived in Bath from Bournemouth coupled in front of 2P 40601. The 2P had been substituted at the last minute for a T9, the rostered loco. The T9 was taken off as shed staff had had difficulty in fitting a tablet catcher. After arrival at Bath, 30932 was turned and despatched light engine to Evercreech Junction where it was turned once again. This was done so that the loco would be facing the right direction to take the excursion, which followed down the line later, back up to London from Templecombe.

The first sighting of a DMU working over the S & D was on May 10 1958 when a Swindon-built 3-car cross-country set formed a Gloucestershire Railway Society railtour. This was followed later in the same month by a Birmingham to Bournemouth excursion (993) comprised of four Derby-built 2-car sets, one unit number being 79145. Another DMU excursion from Birmingham to Bournemouth was in August 1960. This set was formed of a 2-car Metro-Cammell unit plus a 2-car Park Royal unit and a 3-car Metro-Cammell unit. No other instances of diesel multiple units working over the line have come to light, apart from the occasion in December 1965 when a Swindon-built 3-car unit failed at Templecombe station on a Salisbury to Exeter Central train. The set went down to Templecombe shed for attention. Hymek and D63XX class diesels have been noted on track lifting trains after the line's closure. Other excursions have brought somewhat rare locos to Bath (Green Park), such as 6820, *Kingstone Grange*, and 7023, *Penrice Castle*.

The Home Counties Railway Society rail tour of June 7 1964 descending into Bath behind 7F 2-8-0, 53807, and 4F 0-6-0, 44558 (R.E. Toop).

The rare sight of a Castle class loco at Bath (Green Park). 7023, Penrice Castle, *takes the Home Counties Railway Society rail tour north-bound out of Bath* (Derek Cross).

The model

The track plan shown has been drawn to fit a room 12 feet by 8 feet if modelled in 00 gauge. If N gauge is used then a far more accurate representation can be made in the same space. I have built a 00 model very similar to the track plan and can assure readers that the weekday working timetable can be recreated in miniature very closely. The Saturday timetable has not been tried as yet, mainly due to lack of rolling stock, but there would not appear to be any reason why it should not be workable. A club would no doubt be in a better position to supply adequate locos and stock for the increased number of passenger services. A lot depends on the number of fiddle yard tracks which one can fit in. The purists amongst the modelling fraternity might say that the plan sacrifices too much of the original. Nonetheless, to convey the flavour or spirit of a piece of railway is considered just as important as strict accuracy. A layout based on the one drawn will convey that spirit. To model Bath (Green Park) in 00 accurately up to Bath Junction would require at least 36 feet in length and that does not include a fiddle yard.

As drawn, the layout shows an indication of the goods yard and a shunting line. Details of the goods yard and fiddle yards have been omitted for clarity as how the modeller interprets them will depend entirely on what space he has at his disposal. If space were really at a premium the goods yard and shunting line could be left off. Naturally, the lack of complete goods trains would have to be overlooked, but one could still use plenty of non-passenger stock. For example, the pigeon specials and parcels trains conveyed vans of most descriptions. The bonded warehouse could receive individual wagon loads. If space permitted, an elevated coal stage could be built at the engine shed and would entail the use of coal wagons in and out, not forgetting the odd stores van or breakdown train.

Going back to the plan, freights off the S & D could arrive on the shunting line indicated; a very similar action to what would have occurred on the prototype. The train loco could then uncouple, move forward then back down over the cross-overs and make its way to the engine shed. When departing, the shunting engine could assemble the train in the goods yard, pull it forward on to the

Bath (Green Park)

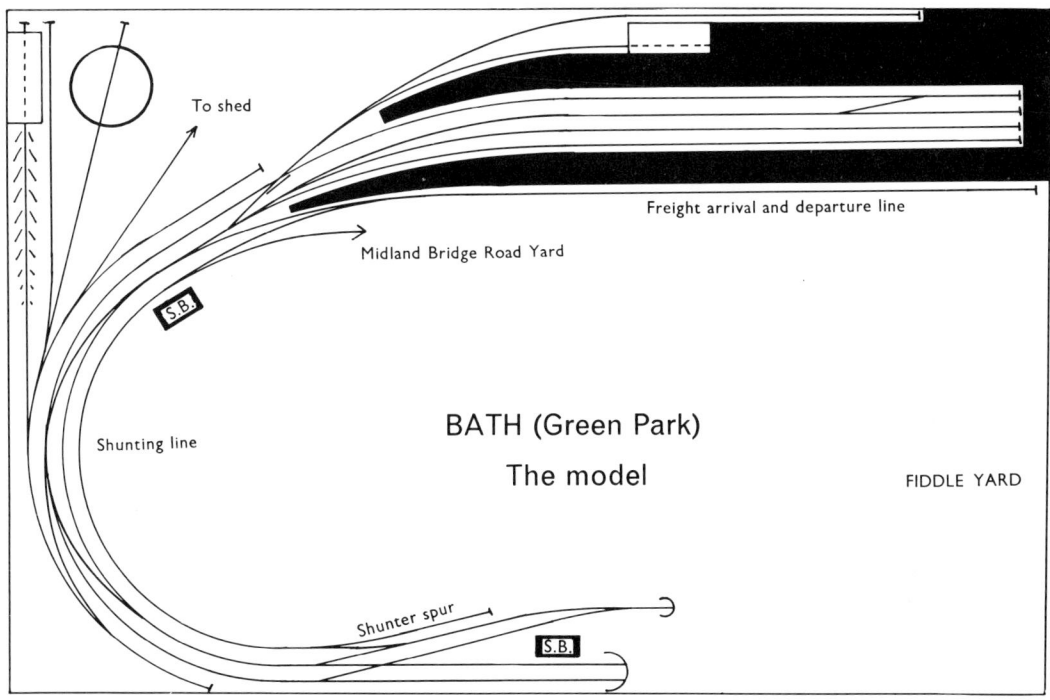

shunting line and then run round the train, ready to bank it up to (the theoretical) Combe Down tunnel. Freights from and to the Midland line could arrive in the line indicated whereupon the shunter would pull the train back on to the shunting line to enable the train loco to reverse back to the engine shed. Not quite such a prototypical movement this, but acceptable under the circumstances.

All passenger train movements, however, can follow the original fairly accurately, although the track layout at the station throat is somewhat different to the prototype. Once again, an attempt has been made to capture the flavour of how things used to be. When planning a layout in 00 gauge it is a good idea to allow a length of 12 inches per coach. The plan shown will accept a double-headed train of six coaches in the south platform. A loco to continue the journey northbound can also be accommodated without fouling any other running line. A six-coach train in 00 is perfectly adequate. The short spur on the run-round adjacent to the north platform should be designed to hold two coaches; the space comes in handy.

Chapter 3

Lyncombe Vale

As soon as southbound S & D trains branched left at Bath Junction they immediately began a climb, mainly 1 in 50, which would take them up to the north end of Combe Down tunnel. Train locos collected the tablet for the single line section to Midford, whilst banker locos on freights collected the 'Bath Banker Staff'. Double track would be regained on the viaduct at Midford. Almost a full 180 degree turn was made in the climb up through the suburbs of Bath. The Western Region main line from Paddington to Bristol was crossed near Oldfield Park. The Co-op siding was passed on a short, level stretch of track. (The method of shunting this siding was mentioned earlier.) A bridge crossed the line as it came up Devonshire bank which became a favourite haunt for photographers. Very shortly trains entered a cutting and disappeared into Devonshire tunnel, emerging on the other side into Lyncombe Vale.

The stretch of track between Devonshire and Combe Down tunnels, known as Lyncombe Vale, would make an ideal setting for a 'watching the trains go by' type layout. Such a layout would be useful at an exhibition with the tracks running to an extensive fiddle yard out of sight of the general public. Once again details of the fiddle yard have been omitted from the track plan as everybody has their own ideas of their layout. Naturally, the more tracks you have, the more trains of differing types can be handled. All the emphasis would be put on making an attractive scene, varying from the embankment on leaving Devonshire tunnel, to the wooded cutting approaching the Combe Down tunnel portal, the small bridge and the platelayer's hut. The extent of the gradient should be visible to the public, making the use of pilot engines or bankers more vivid in the imagination of those not knowledgeable of the S & D grades.

All the train services shown in the Midford section of the working timetable (in the appendices) can be operated, not to mention the odd pigeon special or light engine to add variety. The main operational point of interest of choosing Lyncombe Vale as a site is the use of banking engines up to the mouth of Combe Down tunnel. In later years an ex-GW pannier tank frequently banked freights 'bunker first'. A total of 14 minutes was allowed for the banker to leave Bath and arrive back at the Junction. In model form the banker would have to be geared to run slightly faster than any of the locos which would be likely to haul freight trains. This is because the banker would not be coupled to the train, only buffered up to it to push. The sight of a freight going up the bank with a 4F six inches behind would not be a convincing representation. As a side note of interest just this sort of thing has in fact been known to happen to bankers at other locations in England. Train locos have proved to be stronger than anticipated, leaving the poor banker trying to catch up several feet behind! For an example, see page 60 of *Mendips Engineman*.

If Lyncombe Vale was modelled as an exhibition layout it is suggested that some form of train indicator board be used to keep the public informed of what is happening and what is on its way next. For example, one indicator board (or tape recorded commentary) might say something like: 'The next train to emerge from Combe Down tunnel will be the restaurant car equipped *Pines Express*, hauled by a 2P 4-4-0, piloting a

Lyncombe Vale

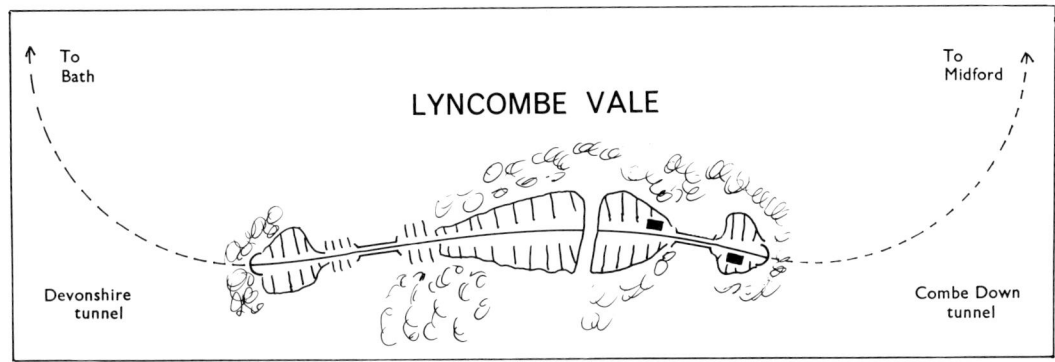

West Country pacific. The train left Bournemouth West earlier this morning at 9.45 am and is due to arrive in Bath at 11.56 am. Its journey north to Manchester will probably continue behind a Stanier Black 5, departure from Bath being at 12.01 pm, etc.' The same idea could be put to good use on all the layouts mentioned in this book. It also adds an air of professionalism to a club layout, as spectators are then assured that the operators really know what they are doing and trying to achieve, as opposed to just sending any old train of coaches or wagons out on the road.

As trains approached Combe Down tunnel from Bath up the 1 in 50 gradient there was a short level stretch before the grade changed to 1 in 100 down, just inside the tunnel. Both Devonshire and Combe Down tunnels had very restricted headroom. In fact, it has been known for the Bath shedmaster to insist that the height of coal in tenders be measured lest it should not go through the tunnels! West Country class pacifics were main culprits of having coal piled high on the tender due partly to their appetite for the stuff. Another reason was that locos on a round trip from Bath to Bournemouth West and return had to have sufficient coal for the complete journey, as there were no coaling facilities at Branksome. Branksome was the servicing/stabling point for S & D locos at the Bournemouth end of the line.

8F 2-8-0, 48737, starts to climb out of Bath on December 30 1963. The coal empties are probably bound for Midsomer Norton (R.E. Toop).

Above *Devonshire bank on August 12 1960 with 7F 2-8-0, 53807, piloting West Country 4-6-2, 34040, Crewkerne, on train M196, the 10.28 am Manchester to Bournemouth West. The angle of the climb out of Bath is most apparent as can be seen from the descending line of houses above the train* (Derek Cross).

Below *2P 4-4-0, 40696, running tender first, pilots 7F 2-8-0, 53808, into Bath on July 2 1960 with the Exmouth to Cleethorpes train. On this occasion the stock is mainly Eastern Region, but the train could be formed of all Southern Region green coaches* (Derek Cross).

Top right *7F 2-8-0, 53806, in its original large boiler condition ascending the 1 in 50 gradient towards Devonshire tunnel on March 10 1952* (R.E. Toop).

Right *A regular sight in Lyncombe Vale was that of south-bound freights being banked up to Combe Down tunnel. On this occasion, March 31 1956, the banking assistance is provided by 4F 0-6-0, 44146* (R.E. Toop).

Below right *The Up* Pines Express *descending towards Bath through Lyncombe Vale, between Combe Down and Devonshire tunnels, on March 12 1957. A typical combination of a 2P and a BR Standard class 5, numbers 40569 and 73052 respectively* (R.E. Toop).

Chapter 4

Midford

Shortly after leaving Combe Down tunnel the small, but nonetheless interesting, station at Midford was reached. It was just over four miles from Bath. The track plan has been drawn to maintain all the essential features of the prototype but the curvature has had to be sharpened because of space restrictions. All the features are somewhat cramped for the same reason; to model Midford accurately in 00 gauge would require an open length of over 32 feet plus fiddle yard. An interesting N gauge track plan featuring Midford appears on page 431 of the December 1980 issue of *Railway Modeller*.

Dropping down the gradients from Combe Down tunnel to Midford station, trains passed a two-siding goods yard on the Down side. This small yard, about a quarter of a mile north of the station, was worked from Midford 'A' ground frame, the frame being released by the single line tablet. The ground frame was operated in consultation with the signalman. Entrance to the yard was through a gate, which was opened to allow wagons to pass. The wagons passed a loading gauge and a six-ton loading crane before entering one of the sidings. A small wooden goods shed was situated by the side of one of these sidings. The station consisted of a range of small, wooden buildings, although the signal box at the southern end of the platform consisted of a timber and glazed superstructure on a stone base. The signal box was reconstructed after an accident in 1936 involving an engine and wagons which got out of control in an incident down the line at Writhlington Colliery. For those interested in the workings of the Midford box, the 'interior' of it has been recreated at the S & D Railway Trust Museum at Washford.

From the goods yard direction the main line then ran under a road bridge, which was more like a short tunnel, being 37 yards in length. The Down 'home' signal and a 'backing signal' were positioned on the bridge. The station itself was set in a picturesque location, being cut into a ledge in the steep hillside. Next to the signal box were a couple of small wooden buildings with rails extending from them. These were used to house small permanent way vehicles. The viaduct commenced immediately beyond the signal box and the track became double about two-thirds along its length. There was another siding on the right-hand Up side of the main line, but it was little used in later years and was removed in 1960. This siding was controlled by Midford 'B' ground frame in consultation with the signalman.

The track plan will enable the modeller to reproduce the daily workings of this small station. (There were around 40 trains per day passing through or stopping during the summer of 1961—see timetable in the appendices.) On weekdays, Midford was served in the Down direction by the Templecombe locals, the 5.58 am and 6.02 pm Bristol Temple Meads to Bournemouth West through trains and the 6.05 pm Bath to Binegar. If you want to stretch a point and tell everyone you are recreating a Thursday in particular, then the 9.03 am Bristol Temple Meads to Bournemouth West through train also called at Midford. This was to drop off pay, which would be conveyed in the travelling safe, for the station staff. In the Up direction all Templecombe locals made a call at the station, together with the 7.33 am Broadstone to Bath and 1.10 pm Bournemouth West to Bristol Temple Meads through train.

Midford

The 6.48 pm Bournemouth West to Bath was also booked to call as and when required.

Only one freight train was booked to call at Midford and that was from 6.05 am to 6.20 am, being the 5.50 am Bath to Templecombe. Midford did not handle much goods traffic so on many days of the week the train would sail by. (An example of how working timetables should not be relied upon for accuracy.) Modeller's licence would no doubt apply here and have the 5.50 am freight call daily. Types of goods traffic included domestic coal, agricultural machinery and 'Fullers Earth'. In post-war years, outgoing freight for Bath and beyond had to be taken down the line to Radstock where it was transferred to an Up train. Likewise, ingoing goods for Midford sped past the yard to be returned on the 5.50 am Down freight from Bath.

Midford had two 'backing signals', one positioned half way along the station platform and a 'repeat arm' positioned on the road overbridge out by the goods yard. These signals were used for any shunting or secondary movement in the 'wrong' direction. A couple of interesting operations using the 'backing signals' can be recreated here. If, for example, a freight train coming from the Evercreech Junction direction found itself short of steam on the steep grades leading to Combe Down tunnel, the driver would make a decision whether or not to continue before actually entering the tunnel. A lineside telephone was provided near the entrance to the tunnel and this would be used by the train crew to advise the signalman at Midford of the train's predicament. The 'backing signals' would then be pulled off. This action authorised the train to reverse back along the line, past the station and out on to the Up line on the viaduct from whence it came a few minutes earlier. The single line section was deemed to be clear once the train had reversed beyond the Up 'inner home' signal. Two courses of action would then be open to the driver. He could sit at the signal and brew up sufficient steam or, as was probably more usual, he could summon a pilot engine from Bath to assist, an unusual movement to keep spectators amused at exhibitions.

The second movement involves the early morning freight and the way in which wagons were occasionally transferred from the goods yard to the siding on the Wellow side of the viaduct. The train would arrive from Bath and stop on the single line adjacent to the goods yard. Wagon brakes would be pinned down and the loco uncoupled. The loco then moved forward, Midford 'A' ground frame being used to set the road for the loco to reverse into

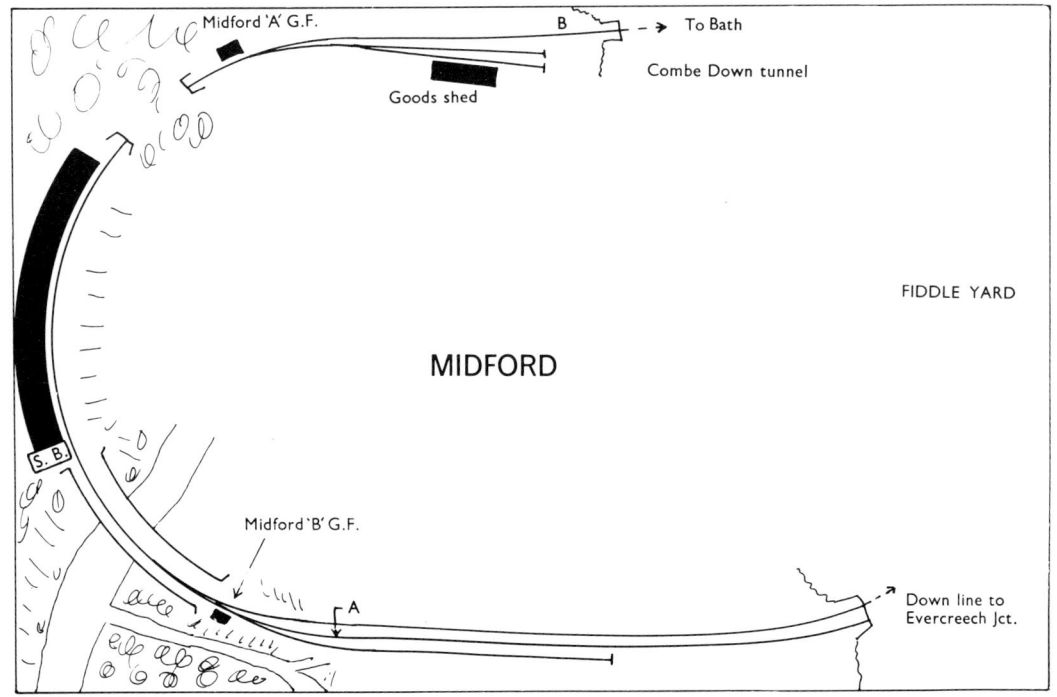

the goods yard. Wagons for transfer were coupled to the loco which then moved out on to the main line and stopped. The ground frame operator then set the road for the loco to push the wagons back beyond the goods yard turnout. Having done this the wagon brakes were pinned down, the loco uncoupled and 'retired' to the goods yard. Once again the road was set for the main line and the brakes were released on the wagons for transfer. These then ran under their own gravity to just beyond the ground frame where they were brought to a halt. The loco then came out of the goods yard and, with the 'backing signals' pulled off, propelled the wagons through the station and across Midford viaduct to the Up siding.

Life for the signalman at Midford could become pretty hectic, particularly on summer Saturdays, as the single track stretch to Bath Junction became something of a bottleneck. Details of a busy summer Saturday in July 1955 appear in Mike Arlett's article, *Summer Saturday at Midford*, published in the November 1981 issue of *Railway World*. This lists not only every train passing Midford, but also details much of the motive power in use. The article provides an interesting comparison of post-war summer traffic over the S & D before the Western Region gained full control.

To give an example of how things worked and the way in which they can be recreated on the model, let us assume that all trains on this Saturday are running to time. Looking at the working timetable in the appendices, it can be seen that the 10.05 am Bournemouth West to Derby was booked to arrive at the Up 'outer home' signal at 12.31 pm. The 7.35 am Nottingham to Bournemouth West would then pass Midford station at 12.34 pm, leaving the section clear for the Derby train by 12.36 pm. On the model this event can be recreated by bringing the Derby train to a stand at point A on the plan, whilst the train from Nottingham runs past. This type of crossing would happen several times on busy summer Saturdays when many 'extras' would be running and trains got out of booked sequence due to late running. On the prototype, point A was roughly the position of the Up 'inner home' signal, so liberties have to be taken here.

If the modeller has sufficient room it would be an idea to include the ex-GWR line which ran between Camerton and Limpley Stoke and passed under the Midford Viaduct. The line closed to passengers in the 1920s but odd freights could be seen up to 1951. A demolition train with a pannier tank at the head ran over the line in 1958. The film entitled *The Titfield Thunderbolt* (1952) was filmed on the branch. The opening sequence showed a West Country class loco hauling a train over the viaduct whilst the branch train passed below. Full details of the filming can be found in the *Railway Magazine* for March 1953, page 163.

Following exceptionally heavy rainfall, a serious landslip occurred on the weekend of December 3/4 1960, due to a collapsed culvert immediately north of the station. This closed the Bath to Radstock section of the line for several days.

Leaving Midford, the line continued southwards passing through the village of Wellow, 6¾ miles from Bath, and Shoscombe and Single Hill Halt at 8½ miles, to arrive outside Writhlington Colliery, 9¾ miles from Bath. This colliery was trip worked from Radstock and remained open to rail traffic well after closure of the S & D to passengers.

Top right *A beautiful view of the south-bound* Pines Express *on July 18 1953 descending towards Midford and crossing Tucking Mill Viaduct soon after leaving Combe Down tunnel. The train is hauled by 3F 0-6-0, 43218, piloting West Country 4-6-2, 34095,* Brentor. *The stock is all in red and cream livery* (R.E. Toop).

Right *2P 4-4-0, 40568, and a Stanier Black 5 about to pass Midford A ground frame on July 25 1953 with the 7.40 am relief from Bournemouth West to Huncoat* (Ivo Peters).

Overleaf *A Birmingham to Bournemouth excursion on May 25 1958, formed by an 8-car DMU, passes Midford A ground frame and the goods yard* (Ivo Peters).

Left *A coal empties train passing Midford station behind 7F 2-8-0, 53805. Notice the 'backing signal' above the loco's right-hand buffer* (Derek Cross).

Above *The 6.05 pm Bath to Binegar arrives at Midford behind Ivatt 2-6-2T, 41243, on August 11 1961. The train is formed of the usual Midland 2-set* (Derek Cross).

Below *Two trains going to and from the Norton Hill Colliery at Midsomer Norton. The locos, 7F 2-8-0, 53808, and 8F 2-8-0, 48737, are passing just south of Midford on July 19 1963* (Derek Cross).

Above 9F 2-10-0, 92233, at Wellow on June 29 1962 with a Bristol Temple Meads to Bournemouth West train (Derek Cross).
Below 2P 4-4-0, 40634, pilots 9F 2-10-0, 92203, with an 11-coach *Pines Express at Wellow in 1962* (Derek Cross).
Bottom BR *Standard class 4 4-6-0, 75073, leaves Wellow with a Templecombe to Bath local on June 29 1962* (Derek Cross).

Chapter 5

Radstock

Radstock, 10¾ miles from Bath (Green Park), was served by the ex-GWR line from Bristol to Frome as well as the ex-S & DJR. A main road from Bath, the A367, had to cross both lines in the middle of the town via level crossings only a short distance apart. The traffic chaos on a summer Saturday can be imagined.

The S & D served a number of collieries in the area, Tynings Colliery in particular being served by a steep gradient. There was a sharp incline where the line to the colliery crossed the S & D which left a very low headroom tunnel on one of the shunting lines. The angle was such that by the time the S & D main lines were crossed there was ample clearance. This low headroom tunnel, known by local railwaymen as the 'Marble Arch', had a clearance of less than 11 feet and so precluded the use of anything but the smallest of locomotives. This is the main reason for choosing Radstock as a good opportunity to use the 0-4-0 Sentinel shunters, 47190 and 47191, also the 0-4-0ST 'Pug', 51202. These diminutive, but nonetheless appealing, locos pottered about the yard during the 1950s, the 'Pug' between 1950 and 1952. 47191 was scrapped in 1959 leaving only 47190 during

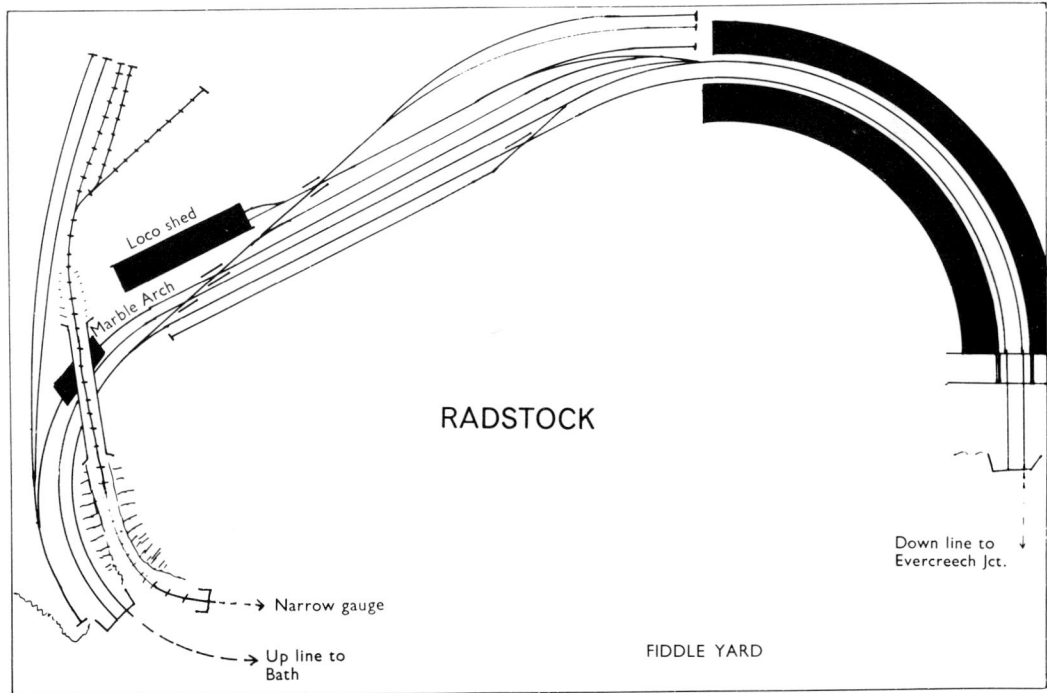

1960. Bath shed records show that she did not work after the summer of 1960 and was scrapped in 1961. The model track plan is more suited to N gauge in a 12 feet by 8 feet room. It has been drawn to enable the use of the 'Pug' and Sentinels, although liberties have been taken with one or two items. For example, on the prototype the loco shed faces the opposite direction. The tracks across the 'Marble Arch' have been designed for narrow gauge only, the point being to have a narrow gauge 'feeder' line from the colliery to the S & D.

Two or three of Bath's Jintys would also be stabled at Radstock. These did trip workings to the various collieries, shunted the yard and performed banking duties on freights bound for the Evercreech Junction direction. These freight trains would arrive in the station platform to await a Jinty to shuffle out from the yard, buffer up to the brake van and exchange two 'crow whistles'. Then, with a combined effort, they would make an attack on the gradients which varied between 1 in 50 and 1 in 300 up to Masbury summit, just over seven miles away. Provision should be made in the fiddle yard for the banker to cross from the Down line to the Up line to enable it to return light engine from Masbury to Radstock.

In the Up direction on weekdays in 1961, Radstock shared the same passenger service as Midford, with the addition of the call by the 3.40 pm Bournemouth West to Bristol Temple Meads in the early evening. The same trains applied in the Down direction but for the addition of the call by the 9.03 am Bristol Temple Meads to Bournemouth West.

During the period of the landslip at Midford, Radstock was used as the terminus for services. Engines from Bournemouth worked up chimney first, returning home tender first. The West Country class were often used. Other locos used on the services would have had steam heating at both ends, although it is thought that a 2P did do one trip—a cold journey for passengers and crew when the loco was running tender first! There was no direct connection between the S & D and the WR lines, although transfer of wagons during the period was possible by way of a colliery yard.

Below Radstock in July 1960, with Jinty 47316 on a coal train. Notice the neat paintwork around the station and the various barrows up against the station building wall (Derek Cross).
Top right A Bath to Evercreech Junction goods train passes Radstock yard with 7F 2-8-0, 53805, at the head. On the extreme right of the picture the low headroom 'Marble Arch' can be seen. The wagons standing under it give an indication of just how low it was (Derek Cross).
Right A view across the engine shed and goods yard at Radstock on April 8 1958. On the left is Jinty 0-6-0T, 47542, and shunting on the right of the picture is Sentinel 0-4-0ST, 47190 (R.E. Toop).
Below right West Country 4-6-2, 34028, Eddystone in its rebuilt condition passes through Radstock with a six-coach train. Notice the SW indicator board and the stonework of the surrounding walls (Derek Cross).

Chapter 6

Midsomer Norton and Norton Hill Colliery

In many people's eyes the most attractive station on the line was Midsomer Norton, 12½ miles out of Bath. The station still exudes a certain atmosphere today even though the bridge over the road to Shepton Mallet has been dismantled, the station buildings are in a derelict condition and stinging nettles grow abundantly in the track bed up to well over platform height. During the 1950s the station regularly won the 'Best kept station' award. A study of the photographs will confirm why.

Midsomer Norton is not only an attractive prototype in the visual sense. Its operational capabilities in model form have just as much appeal. Freight trains passing through between Radstock and Evercreech Junction would often be banked, so the operator has to find a path for the light Jinty to return to Radstock. As mentioned in the previous chapter, a cross-over from Down to Up line must be provided in the fiddle yard for this purpose.

The station was served by several freight trains during the day, mainly to get wagons into and out of Norton Hill Colliery. Access to Norton Hill Colliery was via a trailing turnout off the Down line. The model track plan shows something of a representation of what was actually there, just to make shunting that little more difficult and interesting. The National Coal Board provided their own engines for shunting within the limits of the colliery, although BR locos also performed various operations therein. In 1961, Midsomer Norton had two inbound and outbound services from Bath specifically for coal empties and returning full wagons. Empties were booked to arrive at 9.45 am and 1.27 pm with full wagons going out at 10.40 am and 1.50 pm. A loco roster for the period showed that one loco was booked for both these return trips. As there was no turntable at Midsomer Norton one journey would have to be worked tender first, normally the Midsomer Norton to Bath leg. In 1961, these duties were usually performed by a 7F 2-8-0 in the earlier part of the year or one of the 8F 2-8-0s from around September onwards.

A 1954 appendix for the S & D line stated that Down freights conveying wagons for Norton Hill Colliery should not be brought to a stand on the Down line unless the train had a banking engine at the rear. The remaining wagons not going into the colliery were required to wait outside the Down 'home' signal, secured by their brakes and the assisting engine.

In the case of Up trains, empty wagons for the colliery had to be placed next to the engine. The train would come to a halt at the Up 'home' signal, whereupon the empties

Top right *BR Standard class 4 2-6-4T, 80032, passes Norton Hill Colliery in 1963 with a Bath to Templecombe local. Jinty 47544 stands ready to move out of the colliery road with a train of loaded wagons. The 8F 2-8-0 at the head will take the train on to Bath* (Derek Cross).
Centre right *Jinty 47544 and* Lord Salisbury *engaged in shunting duties at Norton Hill Colliery* (Derek Cross).
Right *The south-bound* Pines Express *passing Midsomer Norton on May 14 1960 behind 2P 4-4-0, 40634, and a BR Standard class 5 loco. On the right is Jinty 47557 which will later attach the vans to north- and south-bound trains as described in the text* (R.E. Toop).

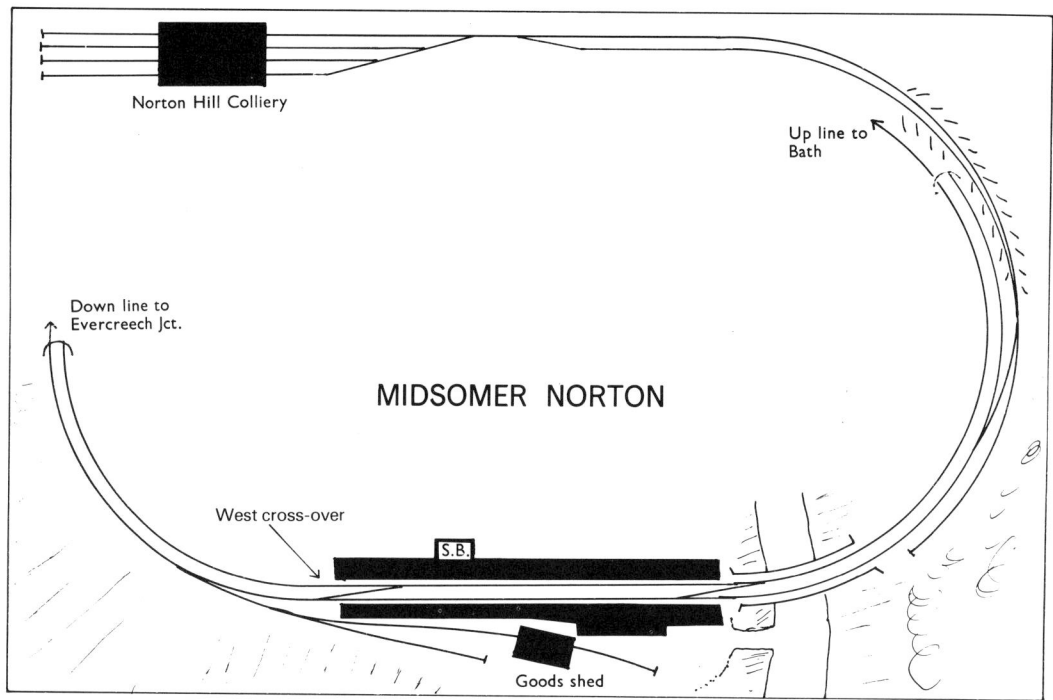

would be uncoupled after the remaining wagons had been secured. The loco and empties ran forward over the West cross-over which was then set to enable reversal to the Down line. The turnout into the colliery was set before the loco was uncoupled from the empties. The loco returned to the Up line via the West cross-over, which was then set in favour of the empties which were allowed to gravitate until they had cleared it. The train engine would once again cross to the Down line and propel the empties through the station into the colliery siding.

The modeller can increase the number of locos that it was possible to see at Midsomer Norton by one if he chooses December 4 1959 as a day worth modelling. On that day, an ex-GW 56XX class 0-6-2T, number 6641, was sent out to Midsomer Norton to work a coal train back to Bath for test purposes. The test was not successful and so the class was not seen again. (An account of the test can be found in Peter Smith's book, *Mendips Engineman*).

It was a Radstock duty to send out a light engine for shunting purposes at Midsomer Norton. One interesting manoeuvre which can be recreated on the model is shown in one of R.E. Toop's photographs. A light engine was rostered to shunt and attach traffic as required to the 1.10 pm from Bournemouth West, 3.20 pm from Bath and 4.15 pm from Templecombe. On the day in question, May 14 1960, Jinty 0-6-0T, 47557, was waiting in the sidings at Midsomer Norton station with fruit vans attached front and rear. When the Down *Pines Express* had cleared the station the loco and wagons came out of the siding and waited at the West cross-over. The 1.10 pm Bournemouth West to Bristol Temple Meads arrived in the station (booked time 3.48 pm). The cross-over was then set for the Jinty to reverse across and attach the rear van to the rear of the train. Once the Bristol-bound train had departed the Jinty followed it out of the station and stopped just beyond the cross-over on the bridge. The 3.20 pm Bath to Templecombe then arrived in the station (booked time 3.57 pm), and the cross-over was set to enable the Jinty to propel the remaining fruit van on to the rear of the train. When the train departed the Jinty was able to continue its other shunting duties.

Leaving Midsomer Norton the line was still climbing at between 1 in 50 and 1 in 300 to pass Chilcompton station, 14½ miles from Bath. Bankers would take water here on their return to Radstock. The once-busy sidings at Moorewood were passed to arrive at Binegar, 17 miles from Bath.

Above *Jinty 0-6-0T, 47557, shunting Midsomer Norton goods yard on May 31 1958* (R.E. Toop).
Below *2P 4-4-0, 40698, arrives at Midsomer Norton in August 1958 with a Templecombe to Bath train* (Derek Cross).

Above *9F 2-10-0, 92206, leaves Midsomer Norton in June 1962 with a Bristol Temple Meads to Bournemouth West train. The four-coach train consists of Midland, Southern and Western Region rolling stock* (Derek Cross).

Below *7F 2-8-0, 53806, stands in the Up platform at Midsomer Norton in July 1960 with a short coal train. Notice the neat and tidy waiting shelter with flower displays* (Derek Cross).

Above BR Standard class 4 4-6-0, 75072, is about to pass Midsomer Norton signal box as it arrives with a Bournemouth West to Bristol Temple Meads train in July 1960. Notice the neatly decorated signal box with its flower displays (Derek Cross).

Below In September 1965 BR Standard class 3 2-6-2T, 82044, leaves Midsomer Norton with Bulleid set number 860 on a Templecombe to Bath working (Derek Cross).

Chapter 7

Binegar

Binegar station has much to offer the modeller. Approaching the station on the Down side were sidings serving the Mendips Stone Works. Although the works did not generate much traffic during the 1950s it has still been included on the model track plan. The goods yard was situated on the Masbury side of the station, again on the Down side of the line. A good space saver for the modeller was that most sidings were served from a dead end headshunt.

Banking locos on passing freight trains on their way up to Masbury picked up a 'Banking Key' from the apparatus at the end of the Down platform. This gave the banker the authority to return from Masbury Summit 'wrong line' to Binegar and regain the Up line via the cross-over at the Evercreech Junction end of the station. Up line freights also stopped at Binegar to detach bankers which had given assistance from Evercreech Junction. Pilots of northbound expresses were sometimes detached at Binegar at busy times. This happened rarely, if at all in 1961, by which time the volume of traffic had declined.

Binegar was served by the same passenger trains as Midford. A special note of operational interest was that this was the terminating station for the 6.05 pm from Bath, arrival time being 6.57 pm. Once the train had arrived and passengers had alighted, the complete train was supposed to run forward, reverse into the Up platform, uncouple and have the loco run round, so that departure was from the Up platform. Invariably, the procedure would be for the loco to uncouple in the Down platform, run round and then depart 'wrong line' crossing to the Up line via the cross-over at the end of the platform.

A regular feature, certainly in 1960 and 1961, was the attachment of horse boxes to the 4.15 pm Templecombe to Bath. The horse boxes contained young calves being transported to Scotland, with as many as four boxes going out on the same train.

Masbury summit, 811 feet above sea level, was reached some 18 miles out from Bath and was the point where banker locos from Radstock would drop away from freights, having made sure that the train's brake van was over the summit. The grade was now downhill through Masbury Halt and Winsor Hill tunnel (see model track plan on page 431 of the December 1980 issue of *Railway Modeller*).

Shepton Mallet was the next station on the line, nearly 22 miles from Bath. Approaching trains crossed two viaducts. The goods yard on the Up side was a spacious affair but was little used in later years. The sidings on the Down side were used for S and T or Permanent Way Department vehicles. Nearly all Down freights were booked to take water here after the heavy up grade work they had just completed.

Evercreech New, 25 miles out of Bath, was a small station which was actually closer to the village than the larger Evercreech Junction station just down the line. The goods yard on the Down side was served by a trip working from Evercreech Junction, mainly to get Conflats and box vans there for the use of a local milk machinery manufacturer.

Right *2P 4-4-0, 40698, has just arrived at Binegar on July 8 1958 with a Bath to Templecombe local. Note the banker engine tablet apparatus in the middle foreground* (Derek Cross).

S.B.
Goods shed
BINEGAR
Mendips
Stone
Works
Down line to
Evercreech Jct.
FIDDLE YARD
Up line to
Bath

40698

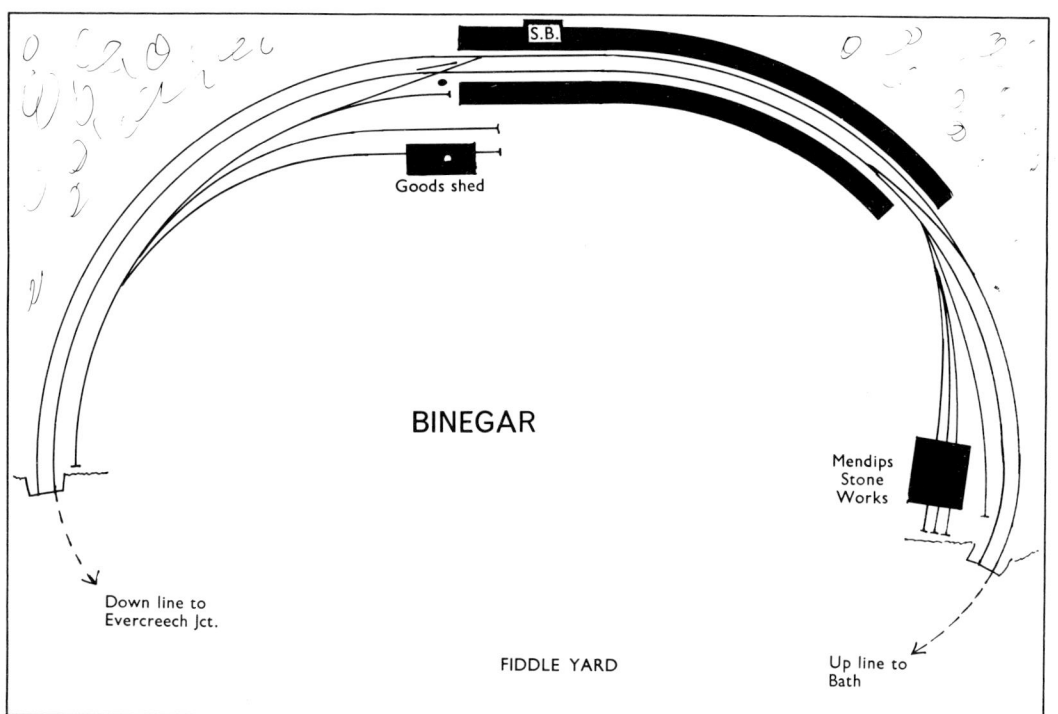

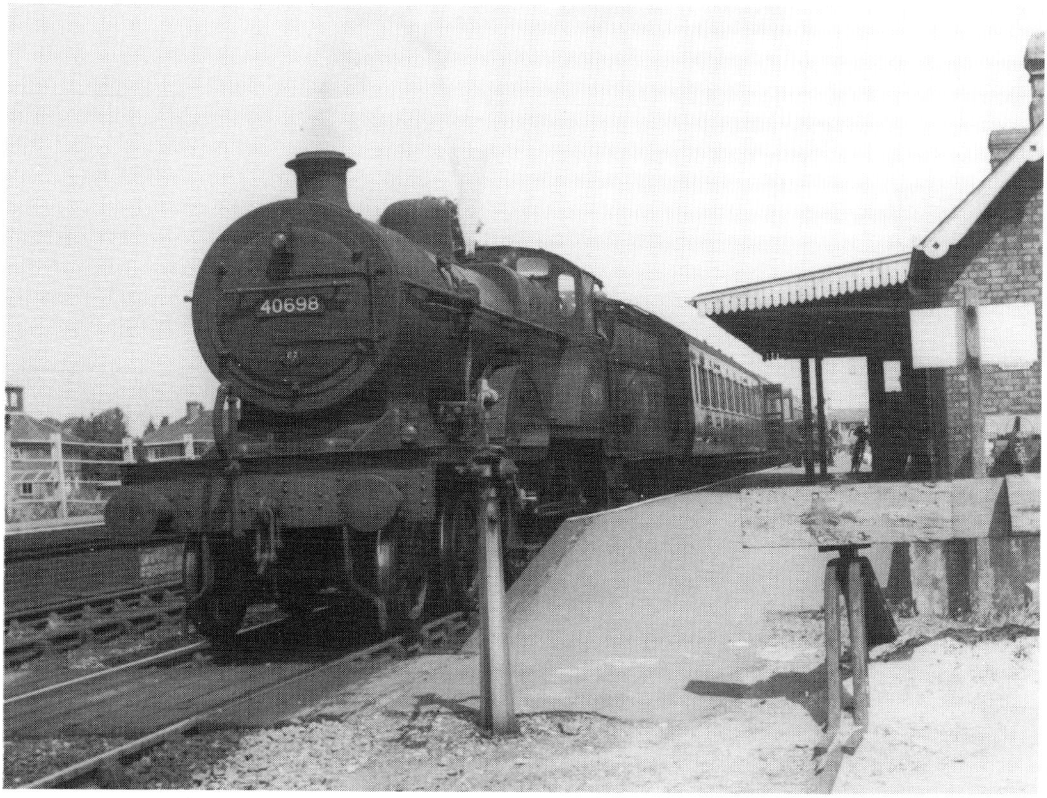

Top left 7F 2-8-0, 53805, passes Binegar in July 1960 with a short, seven-wagon freight on its way from Bath to Evercreech Junction. Short freights such as this were not uncommon on the S & D in later years. A good excuse for modellers who are short of space or rolling stock (Derek Cross).

Left On July 12 1961 4F 0-6-0, 44422, arrives at Binegar with a Templecombe to Bath local (Derek Cross).

Below left The Exmouth to Cleethorpes train of August 12 1961 approaches Binegar hauled by 22XX 0-6-0, 3210, and 7F 2-8-0, 53806. This combination of classes was an unusual occurrence, but it just goes to show that anything was possible on a summer Saturday on the S & D (Derek Cross).

Above The Bournemouth West to Sheffield train of August 12 1961 passes Binegar signal box behind 2P 4-4-0, 40564, and 7F 2-8-0, 53810. Note that photographs of this train and the Cleethorpes train heading north out of Bath appear earlier in the book under the 'Summer Saturday' section (Derek Cross).

Below 7F 2-8-0, 53808, (now preserved) leaves the goods yard at Shepton Mallet and joins the Up line on its way to Bath in June 1960. Notice the concrete sleepers of the Down line. In the distance the bridge carrying the ex-GWR line between Wells and Witham can be seen (Derek Cross).

Chapter 8

Evercreech Junction and 'the branch' services

The station at Evercreech Junction, 26½ miles from Bath, was one of the busiest stations on the S & D line, this being the junction for the Highbridge branch. In 1961 all passenger trains were booked to call at the station, weekday trains as well as those of summer Saturdays only. During the 1950s the only exception to this rule was the summer Saturday 7.43 am from Birmingham New Street to Bournemouth West. This train stopped at Shepton Mallet to detach the pilot and passed through Evercreech Junction non-stop (booked passing time 11.33 am), before calling at Wincanton. The pilot engine subsequently followed the express light engine to Evercreech Junction where it would be turned and made ready to pilot a northbound express back over the Mendips. All freight trains were also booked either to stop and take water at the station or to be shunted and remarshalled in one of the yards. Shunting in the yards on weekdays was almost a 24-hour-a-day job, until the gradual decline in freight traffic.

The station and yards were spread over a large area but, nonetheless, an acceptable reduction for modelling purposes can be made to fit the whole affair into a space 20 feet by 12 feet in 00 gauge. The track plan shows that the number of sidings has been reduced, the turntable has been moved to the other side of the line and the station itself has been built on a sharp curve as opposed to the gentle curve of the original. Also on the model plan, use has been made of a space-saving double-slip point to connect the middle sidings with the Up line and the station goods yard. On the prototype, the double-slip was actually two separate turnouts. Subject to the number of fiddle yard roads which the modeller is able to accommodate, it should be possible to recreate a whole day's traffic in the station. The following paragraphs describe what could have been a typical weekday at the Junction in mid-summer 1961, assuming that all trains were running on schedule according to the working timetable. Various notes have been added where modeller's licence has been allowed to alter the happenings slightly. Reference should be made to the timetable transcription in the appendices.

The first train of the day was the 2.40 am Freight and Mail from Bath which arrived in the Down platform at 4.39 am. The loco was rostered for the *Pines* diagram (SX during the summer service) so the use of a 9F or a Standard class 5 is in order here. Prior to 1954 the West Country class was normally used. The loco would take water from the column near the level crossing whilst the local postman unloaded any mail for his area from the vans marshalled at the front of the train. Departure was at 4.50 am.

Shortly after, the 4.20 am Freight from Templecombe would arrive at the Up 'home' signal at 4.52 am and the loco would take water. On Mondays only the train would be double-headed. This was to get a shunter to the yards from Templecombe after the weekend lull in traffic. This loco would go into the yards light engine whilst the train loco was taking water. Locos used for the duty were usually 3Fs or 22XX. Having taken water, the train would then move forward through the station, on to the Highbridge branch line and reverse into the Up yard, where it would shunt as required. The train sometimes conveyed empty milk tanks from Templecombe to Evercreech Junction where they would be detached for later attachment to

Evercreech Junction

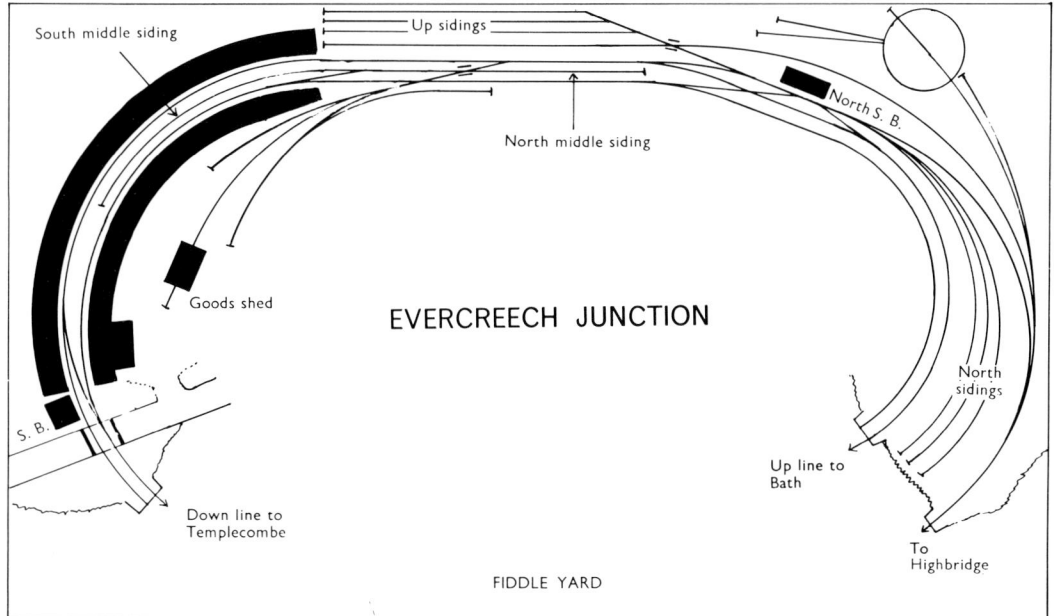

the 8.15 am Evercreech Junction to Highbridge. The tanks were subsequently worked back from Highbridge to the milk factory at Bason Bridge. The freight from Templecombe was allowed just over one hour to marshal its train before forming the 6.05 am Freight up the branch to Highbridge, where arrival time was booked at 7.53 am.

Whilst the Templecombe to Highbridge freight was shunting in the yard the 3.30 am Freight from Bath to Evercreech Junction would arrive on the Down main line. On the model this arrival point would be possibly around the middle of the Down platform, depending on the number of wagons in the train. A 'backing signal', the same as those at Midford, was positioned at the cross-over leading from the Down line to the Highbridge branch. On the prototype Down freights would not pass the Down 'home' signal as this would mean that the train was in the South Box section and a 'wrong line order' would be needed to reverse. Wagons for the Highbridge branch would usually be marshalled at the rear of the Down freight. The loco of the Templecombe to Highbridge freight would, if needed, come across from the Up yard to the rear of the freight and couple up to the wagons for Highbridge. The 'backing signal' would be pulled off to give it authority to reverse across the Up line and on to the branch whence it would propel the wagons on to the waiting Highbridge train in the Up yard.

Once this operation was completed the 'backing signal' would come off once more and the remainder of the 3.30 am from Bath would reverse direct into the North sidings. The loco then went to the turntable and made ready to return to Bath with the 6.25 am Freight. Freight locos often had an 'out and back' type roster.

At 6.20 am a light engine from Templecombe was booked to arrive at the North Box. This loco was to work the 6.35 am Freight from Evercreech Junction as far as Poole and was almost without exception alloted to 4F 44102 up to the early 1960s. She was not equipped with steam heating so was kept away from passenger trains except in summer when heavy demands were made on motive power. The 6.25 am Freight for Bath would depart from the Up sidings. Bath-bound freights were banked when required as far as Binegar. At 6.35 am the Poole freight would depart from the North sidings, always with a brake van at both ends of the train. This was because of the working arrangement at Templecombe, described later in the Templecombe chapter.

Between 7.00 am and 8.30 am Templecombe- and Bath-bound freights visited the yards. The Templecombe to Bath train would go directly on to the Highbridge branch before reversing into the Up sidings, whilst the arrival from Bath would go through the 'backing signal' procedure. At 7.23 am the

7.00 am from Templecombe arrived in the Up platform. This train was usually formed of a Midland 2-set and a SR 3-set. Departure was at 7.25 am. On a Monday morning during the summer, a Standard 5 or a 7F 2-8-0 might be used to get it back to Bath and change over with a Templecombe engine which may have finished up at Bath on the Saturday.

The first of the Highbridge branch trains arrived at the Junction at 7.56 am. This was the 7.00 am from Highbridge. During the 1950s, this would be a 1P 0-4-4T or a 3F with a Midland 2-set. In the 1960s the 22XX class, the Ivatt 2-6-2Ts, BR Standard class 3 2-6-2Ts and WR pannier tanks could be seen with a B set or, in later years, a single Hawksworth coach. Other WR non-corridor stock has been noted. For a short time in 1960, Stanier class 3 2-6-2Ts were used on branch services, numbers 40098, 40126 and 40171 in particular. 40161 also did one trip before failing a boiler inspector's examination. Once the branch train had arrived and its passengers alighted, there were two methods of running round the coaches of this train which were employed. The first was to uncouple the loco, run forward over the level crossing, reverse on to the Up line and come back to the Down line via the cross-overs in the middle sidings. The loco coupled up to the coaches, took them back through the middle siding cross-overs to the Up line and finally reversed into the Up platform. The other method was for the complete train to move across the level crossing from the Down platform, set back across the cross-over to the Up platform, uncouple and have the loco run round via the Down platform and middle siding cross-overs.

All this was done in readiness to make connection with the 5.58 am Bristol Temple Meads to Bournemouth West through train, which arrived in the Down platform at 8.05 am. The loco took water here, departure being nine minutes later at 8.14 am. The Highbridge train then departed from the Up platform at 8.15 am, not forgetting that on occasions it could convey empty milk tankers. The Midland 2-sets were often marshalled so that the guard's compartment was near to the middle of the train.

The working timetable stated that a light engine was due to go through the station from the yards around 8.32 am on its way to shunt Wincanton. In practice, this loco would depart somewhat earlier and was usually back in Templecombe shed by 8.30 am. The loco would often stop and take water in the station on its way to Wincanton.

The 8.20 am local from Templecombe arrived in the Up platform at 8.46 am. This

The northern end of Evercreech Junction. The Highbridge branch disappears into the middle distance whilst the double track curves away to the right in the Bath direction. Notice the 'backing signal' on the right of the picture (Peter Pike).

train was usually a Midland 2-set, which had formed the Templecombe to Bailey Gate the day before, with a PMV attached at the rear. The PMV would work back to Templecombe later in the 4.19 pm Highbridge to Templecombe milk and perishables train. The 8.20 am was mainly patronised by school children who alighted at Cole. Once the passengers had alighted, the train ran forward and then reversed up to the buffers in the south middle siding. Empty water cans from Bruton Road crossing were picked up by this train and usually carried in the guard's compartment, or sometimes on the loco's buffer beam.

At 9.28 am the 7.33 am Broadstone to Bath called at the Up platform, whilst the 8.15 am Bath to Templecombe called at the Down platform. (On summer Saturdays the 8.15 am Down was double-headed to get a pilot to the Junction to assist a northbound express back to Bath.) Any parcels for Evercreech Junction and the Highbridge branch were unloaded from the vans at the head of the 8.15 am. These vans, it may be remembered, were attached to the 8.15 am off the Leicester parcels train at Bath. Once the Bath- and Templecombe-bound trains had departed around 9.30 am, the loco and 2-set to form the 9.55 am to Highbridge came out of the middle siding. If heavy or numerous parcels had been taken off the Templecombe local for onward transmission to the Highbridge branch then the loco and 2-set would first reverse back into the Down platform and collect the parcels. The train then went through the cross-overs of the middle siding to the Up line and reversed into the Up platform ready to depart at 9.55 am. There was no facility for Highbridge trains to depart from the Down platform.

In the 1950s a trip freight from Templecombe arrived around 10.20 am. The loco off this train shunted the station yard before going back to Templecombe with the 11.20 am Trip Freight. In later years the station yard was shunted as required.

The pilot for the Up *Pines Express* arrived light engine from Templecombe at 10.35 am and reversed directly to the buffers in the south middle siding. The 5.50 am Freight from Bath to Templecombe arrived at 10.35 am. When this train had shunted it departed around 11.40 am. One of the photographs shows this train having collected the full water cans for Bruton Road crossing.

The Up platform then saw the arrival of the 10.20 am from Templecombe at 10.43 am, usually a Southern Region 3-set or 3-set plus strengthening coach in the summer. This was the stock off the 8.15 am Bath to Templecombe. For modelling purposes which will become apparent shortly, this train can be hauled by 3F 43436. One minute later, at

3F 0-6-0, 43218, shunting in the Up sidings at Evercreech Junction on May 30 1959 (R.E. Toop).

10.44 am, the 9.45 am Highbridge to Templecombe arrived in the Down platform. This train was usually composed of two 2-sets, either Midland pattern or Western Region B sets. On arrival at Templecombe one set would remain in the station area to form the 3.35 pm Templecombe to Bailey Gate, whilst the other set went down to Templecombe Lower yard to return to the Junction later as the 12.30 pm empty stock from Templecombe Lower.

When the Highbridge to Templecombe train departed at 10.47 am this left the Down line clear for the loco off the 10.20 am from Templecombe to run round its coaches and then shunt them to the buffers of the north middle siding. Of interest here is the fact that this buffer stop was fitted with a three-link coupling. This was attached to the stock to prevent it running away down grade. If, as suggested earlier, use is made of 3F 43436, this loco can then go over to the Up yard to haul the 11.06 am Freight to Highbridge. 43436 was a regular on the 11.06 am during the 1950s. This train conveyed water cans on the loco's buffer beam.

At 11.03 am both the Up *Pines Express* (9.45 am off Bournemouth West) and the 9.03 am Bristol Temple Meads to Bournemouth West were occupying the platforms. The 9.03 am was double-headed as far as Shepton Mallet on summer Saturdays where the pilot loco was detached. The pilot arrived light engine at the Junction a few minutes later in readiness to pilot a northbound express after turning on the turntable. The pilot was detached at Shepton Mallet because of the traffic complications which could occur at the Junction if, for any reason, the *Pines Express* could not clear the Up line to enable the pilot to get out of the way of the Bournemouth-bound train. As soon as the *Pines* arrived, the pilot engine sitting in the south middle siding would promptly move out on to the Up line and back down on to the train in the Up platform. Departure was at 11.06 am and would make a fine sight on a model if it passed the North Box at the same time as the 11.06 am Freight to Highbridge went up the branch. This action was often seen on the prototype as the two trains departed.

At 11.49 am the 5.50 am Bath to Templecombe was booked to go through the station and, as mentioned earlier, would usually collect two or three full water cans on the buffer beam. The 12 noon Templecombe to Bath local called at the Up platform between 12.20 and 12.21 pm, being followed by the arrival at 12.51 pm of a Midland 2-set or a B set as empty stock from Templecombe Lower. This loco and stock immediately shunted to the south middle siding, and waited to make connection with the 11.40 am Bournemouth West to Bristol Temple Meads, due in at 1.02 pm. Once that train had departed, the loco and stock to form the 1.15 pm to Highbridge came out of the south middle siding and backed down into the Up platform.

The next sequence of events was usually for the 11.00 am Freight from Bath to arrive and set back into the North sidings by 1.10 pm. The Highbridge train then departed at 1.15 pm, normally passing the 7.38 am Freight from Highbridge around West Pennard, even though this train was booked to arrive at the Junction at 1.02 pm. This was another freight which could be seen carrying water cans on the buffer beam. At 1.50 pm a freight departed to Bath from the Up sidings and shortly after, at 2.07 pm, a freight from Templecombe arrived and set back into the Up sidings. The 1.10 pm Bath to Templecombe called at the Down platform between 2.24 pm and 2.27 pm to be followed down the line by the 2.35 pm Freight back to Templecombe from the North sidings. At 3.04 pm the 1.10 pm Bournemouth West to Bristol Temple Meads called at the Up platform. This train was usually a Western Region set of stock with a 76XXX loco at the head. At 3.19 pm the 2.20 pm Highbridge to Templecombe called at the Down platform, normally a Midland 2-set or a B set, and continued on its way at 3.24 pm.

A light engine, running tender first, arrived at the Junction from Templecombe at 3.35 pm. This was the loco off the 1.10 pm from Bath and it went direct to the stock sitting in the north middle siding and coupled up. After the 2.00 pm Freight from Bath had arrived in the North sidings at 3.53 pm, the yard shunter took a trip freight up the line to Evercreech New, mainly for the benefit of the milk machinery manufacturer there. Conflats and box wagons were the usual traffic.

As the trip freight went up the line it would pass the southbound *Pines Express* making its way down to a 4.05 pm arrival time at the Junction. The *Pines* pilot loco was taken off at the Junction and, depending on the train's time keeping, would move forward over the level crossing and set back into the Up platform. The *Pines* was booked to depart at

4.10 pm, the pilot at 4.18 pm, after crossing back to the Down line and following the 4.16 pm Evercreech Junction to Bournemouth West train. Alternatively, if the *Pines* arrived three or four minutes early at the Junction, the pilot would immediately depart light engine, ahead of the express, to Templecombe. As soon as the *Pines Express* had departed at 4.10 pm, the loco and stock from the north middle siding pulled into the Down platform to form the 4.16 pm Evercreech Junction to Bournemouth West. This train formed a connecting service to intermediate stations for passengers off the *Pines*. If the *Pines* was running, say, up to half an hour late, the 4.16 pm would be held at the Junction. If the *Pines* was running extremely late, for example, in bad winter weather or on a busy summer Saturday, the 4.16 pm would be despatched and a 'scratch' train formed to fill the breach. During the mid 1950s the station master at Evercreech Junction, Mr Pike, pestered the authorities into letting him have a couple of spare coaches for emergency use such as when trains were running late and passengers needed to make connections at Templecombe. The coaches he was given were two ex-LSWR re-builds, numbers 2626 and 4654. Full details of these two coaches can be found in the Oakwood Press books concerning Maunsell coaches. They were both withdrawn in 1959 and replaced for a time by a single red and cream livery Midland Region corridor coach and a van.

Another 2-set (Midland or B set) arrived in the Up platform at 4.29 pm from Templecombe. This was the return working of the stock of the 2.20 pm Highbridge. Once unloaded it shunted to the south middle siding. Bath to Templecombe and Templecombe to Bath locals crossed each other around 4.40 pm. Once the Up platform became vacant, the 2-set positioned itself to form the 5.00 pm departure to Highbridge. The trip working from Evercreech New arrived back at 4.45 pm and cleared the branch for the arrival of the 4.00 pm from Highbridge to arrive in the Down platform just as the 5.00 pm to Highbridge was departing.

The train which had arrived from Highbridge then took up position in the south middle siding and made connection with the 3.35 pm Bristol Temple Meads to Bournemouth West, the 3.40 pm Bournemouth West to Bristol Temple Meads and the 4.37 pm Bath to Templecombe, before departing from the Up platform as the 6.02 pm to Highbridge. Nearly an hour would then pass by before the next train was due and that was the 4.19 pm Milk and Perishables train from Highbridge to Templecombe at 6.56 pm. Usual motive power was a 3F or a

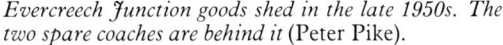

Evercreech Junction goods shed in the late 1950s. The two spare coaches are behind it (Peter Pike).

22XX. This train sometimes conveyed as many as 10 milk tanks to Templecombe which would then be sent to London via the Southern Region. At 7.01 pm a freight from Templecombe was booked to arrive in the Up sidings, followed at 7.20 pm by a freight departure to Bath.

The station then had another quiet spell until 8.09 pm when the 7.10 pm from Highbridge arrived in the Down platform. This train conveyed perishables vans on the rear which would be attached to the Templecombe to Derby perishables, due in the Up platform at 8.47 pm. The loco off the Highbridge train had to do some fairly prompt shunting to get things as ready as possible for the perishables train. First, the loco would run round the complete train and buffer up to the vans at the rear. It would then pull the whole train back across the middle siding cross-overs and position the two coaches up against the buffers in the south middle siding. The loco then had to shunt the vans into a pre-arranged order to make life easy for the perishables loco to attach. These vans were then shunted up to the two coaches and the loco moved back to wait in the north middle siding. In the middle of all this the Down platform had to be clear at 8.21 pm for the 6.02 pm Bristol Temple Meads to Bournemouth West. In the early 1950s the perishables train was worked by Ivatt 2-6-0 4MTs, followed by 4Fs and Standard class 4 4-6-0s. At 8.34 pm the 2.40 pm Freight from Highbridge arrived in the North sidings and shunted ready to depart at 9.00 pm to Templecombe.

The 8.25 pm Perishables train from Templecombe to Derby was booked to arrive at 8.47 pm. Every effort would be made to run a perishables train to time because of the nature of what it was carrying. The train loco would attach the wagons from the middle siding, sometimes having to make drastic rearrangements to the formation of the train, depending on ultimate destinations of the vans being carried. Another problem was that a rule stated that four-wheeled vans should not be at the rear of the train and the last vehicle should be fitted with a guard's type hand brake. When time was tight, this rule was sometimes disregarded! In later years, the train was usually hauled by a Standard class 5. If, for any reason, the train was over the maximum load laid down for the train engine, the yard shunter would be pressed into service to assist the train as far as Binegar.

Just after the perishables departed at 9.04

The Evercreech Junction level crossing gates swing open to allow road traffic to pass. The gates had been shut for a few minutes whilst 2P 4-4-0, 40634, arrived piloting BR Standard class 5 4-6-0, 73052, on the Down Pines Express *on June 1 1957. The 2P had uncoupled, run forward and then reversed back to the Up platform via the crossover whilst the Standard 5 took water* (R.E. Toop).

pm the Highbridge to Templecombe freight was booked to call at the Down platform and take water. Whilst this was happening the 6.48 pm Bournemouth West to Bath would call at the Up platform between 9.13 pm and 9.15 pm. The loco and 2-set sitting in the south middle road made connection with the Bath train and departed from the Up platform at 9.25 pm, the last train of the day over the Highbridge branch. If milk traffic demanded then the 6.48 pm would convey empty milk tanks from Templecombe, detach them in the platform at Evercreech Junction for collection and transportation up the branch by the 9.25 pm.

If running, the 'when required' 8.55 pm Bath to Templecombe freight called at the Down platform to take water. At 11.05 pm the 8.10 pm Freight from Poole to Bath (SX during the summer service) arrived in the Up sidings. This was the fourth leg for the loco rostered to the *Pines* diagram (SX during the summer service). A good opportunity to use a 9F or a Standard 5 on a little shunting before departure at 11.30 pm. (If pre-1954 is being modelled, use can also be made of a West Country.) The final booked train of the day was the 10.25 pm Bath to Templecombe. This ran as a passenger train to Shepton Mallet and then as a 'stop as requested' train from there to Templecombe. It would usually go through Evercreech Juncton non-stop. On Friday nights in the summer this two-coach train would sometimes be hauled by a 7F needing to get to Templecombe to work the northbound Exmouth to Cleethorpes from Templecombe to Bath the next day. On these occasions, the loco would detach and turn on the turntable before continuing the journey to Templecombe tender first. This was done at Evercreech Junction as the Templecombe turntable was too small for a 7F.

On summer Saturdays most freight trains were cancelled to enable the holiday expresses to run. Pilots for these trains in the northbound direction arrived at Evercreech Junction either piloting southbound trains or as light engines coupled in twos or threes from Templecombe. The pilot engines would line up in the south middle siding and at busy times other pilots would have to find refuge in the station goods yard. When a train from Bath which was booked to call at Templecombe Upper was piloted by a Templecombe engine, the pilot would not detach at Evercreech Junction but would continue with the train down to Templecombe. The Highbridge branch ran the same service on Saturdays, even including the two Up and Down freights. The 4.00 pm from Highbridge, however, was extended to Templecombe.

A mention can be made here with regard to certain unusual occurrences. About once a year the Inspector's Saloon would make a journey over the branch from Highbridge down to Evercreech Junction. This job was usually a 3F turn but, in February 1956, small prairie 5522 put in an appearance. Weed killing trains were another feature of the line every once in a while. At various times during school holidays special trains were run between Templecombe and Burnham-on-Sea. Burnham-on-Sea had been closed to regular passenger services in October 1951. Also in the late 1950s and early 1960s a Sunday special would run about twice a year from Highbridge to Bournemouth and return. To add a final variety to motive power used on branch passenger services, one can use the 2P 4-4-0s if modelling 1956. For two or three months of that year Highbridge shed found itself temporarily short of locos, so the 2Ps filled in as and when required.

The station at Cole, 29¼ miles from Bath, would make an attractive model. It was served by the majority of passenger trains but by only one freight train in 1961. That was the 5.50 am Bath to Templecombe. The three-road goods yard did not handle much traffic, apart from the odd wagon of coal for the local merchant. Up to the mid-1950s bacon was despatched regularly.

The S & D crossed the Paddington to Exeter main line not far north of Cole and was, in fact, visible from the station. If the modeller wanted to stretch a point it would no doubt be in order to think of Cole being somewhat closer to the WR main line than it actually was. What an assortment of locos and rolling stock this would permit!

A little further down the line the town of Wincanton was reached, 33½ miles from Bath. The station enjoyed a good passenger service as well as several calls by freight trains. The yard was also shunted by the light engine discussed in the Evercreech Junction chapter on its way back to Templecombe. The main traffic was coal wagons but the odd milk tanker found its way in occasionally, for use by the milk processing factory. Powdered milk was despatched in box vans, whilst cattlefeed and fertilizers were ingoing traffic.

Above *A regular sight during the summer of 1962 was BR Standard class 4 4-6-0s, 75023 and 75027, working the 11.12 am Bournemouth West to Sheffield train. The pair are seen here departing from Evercreech Junction on September 1 1962. 22XX 0-6-0, 3206, is waiting in the south middle siding prior to working the 1.20 pm up the branch to Highbridge* (Roy Bullock).

Below *Evercreech Junction station Up platform station buildings. These would make an ideal model together with the attractive flower garden areas* (Peter Pike).

Evercreech Junction

Above *In June 1960 7F 2-8-0, 53810, pauses at the Evercreech Junction Down platform to pick up the water cans seen on the buffer beam. The train is the 5.50 am freight from Bath to Templecombe. The south middle siding can be clearly seen. The Up sidings are in the top left-hand corner of the picture. This view gives some idea of the gradients involved* (Derek Cross).

Below *3F 0-6-0, 43216, waits in the south middle siding to form an Evercreech Junction to Highbridge train on June 29 1962. Notice the petrol car and trolley on the left of the picture* (Derek Cross).

Above *BR Standard class 4 4-6-0, 75027, arrives with a Bath-bound train and makes connection with the Highbridge train on June 29 1962. Notice the driver and fireman of the branch train taking a meal break on the edge of the Down platform. An action which is not advisable anywhere on today's railway with High Speed Trains!* (Derek Cross).

Below *West Country pacific, number 34043,* Combe Martin, *hauling the* Pines Express *between Cole and Wincanton during the summer of 1962. Notice the Midland, Western and BR Mk 1 coaching stock* (G.A. Richardson).

Above *0-6-0PT, 4631, in June 1965 with a Highbridge to Templecombe train. This was a typical formation for the branch train in its final years* (Derek Cross).

Below *Another June 1965 shot of the branch train leaving the Up platform at Evercreech Junction behind Ivatt 2-6-2T, 41243* (Derek Cross).

Above *A sad day at Evercreech Junction. The last Down* Pines Express, *hauled by 9F 2-10-0, 92220,* Evening Star, *takes water on September 8 1962.* (Roy Bullock).

Above *On June 30 1962 22XX 0-6-0, 3206, leaves Cole with a Highbridge to Templecombe train. Notice the three-way turnout in the small goods yard* (Derek Cross).
Below *3F 0-6-0, 43218, near Cole with a Highbridge to Templecombe milk train* (R.C. Riley).

Chapter 9

Templecombe

The S & D line made connection with the Southern Region Waterloo to Exeter main line 37 miles from Bath at Templecombe. A track plan has been included to illustrate the interesting and complex movements which took place, but it should be noted that it is a *sketch plan* only and has many tracks omitted for clarity. Detailed track and signalling plans can be found in the Oxford Publishing Company's book, *Historical Survey of the Somerset and Dorset Railway*. The layout at Templecombe would be extremely difficult to model, requiring a vast area, even in N gauge. Nevertheless, Templecombe still warrants inclusion in this book because of the unusual, if not unique way in which trains worked in and out of the station.

An interesting example of train working concerns the way in which the 6.48 am Bath to Bournemouth West combined with the 7.33 am from Broadstone at Templecombe Upper on weekdays. The train from Broadstone would come up the S & D, past Templecombe Lower platform and come to a stand near A. *(NB The distance between A and B on the plan was much greater in reality.)* A pilot engine would then drop down from the Templecombe Upper line and attach itself to the rear of the waiting train. Having done this the complete train, with locos at both ends, would cross to the Down line at B and climb the 1 in 100 gradient to Templecombe Upper platform and stop near C. The pilot loco uncoupled and disappeared into the Upper sidings to perform other duties. The train loco would then push the stock back out to one of the sidings. A few minutes later, the 6.48 am train from Bath came up the gradient from the junction and stopped near C. Whilst passengers were getting on and off the train, the loco and stock of the Broadstone to Bath train would come out of the sidings and pass the train in the platform on the adjacent road and come to halt clear of the cross-over at E. The cross-over was then set for the loco and coaches to set back from the Up line to Down and couple up with the coaches in the platform. At 9.05 am the two combined trains moved out of the platform, crossing again to the Up line at E, to descend the bank and come to a halt near A. Here the trains were uncoupled, the Broadstone to Bath train continuing north on the Up line and the Bournemouth train going south through the cross-over at B to gain the single line through Templecombe Lower platform.

On summer Saturdays during the late 1950s and early 1960s, when departure times of the two trains were altered, a somewhat different set of operations was carried out. The Bath-bound train, which on Saturdays originated from Bournemouth West at 7.12 am, arrived as usual at A and awaited a pilot to haul it back up to the Upper platform at C. The pilot loco did not then uncouple as it did during the week. Instead the train, with a loco at both ends, moved off into the sidings. With the platform now clear, the 6.48 am from Bath arrived as usual near C. As passengers were boarding and alighting, the Bournemouth to Bath train with locos at both ends came out of the sidings, past the train in the platform, coming to a halt clear of the cross-over at E. Once the cross-over was set the locos and coaches set back from the Up line to the Down and buffered up to the rear of the Bournemouth-bound train sitting in the platform. The scene was then train loco, coaches, pilot, coaches and train loco. The

Templecombe

pilot uncoupled from the Bath-bound coaches and coupled up to the rear of the Bournemouth-bound train.

At 9.15 am the Bournemouth West to Bath train departed from the Upper platform, crossing from the Down line to the Up at the cross-over at E, leaving the Bournemouth West bound train behind. This subsequently departed at 9.28 am, following the same path down to A where the train came to a stand. The pilot on the Bath end of the train was uncoupled, leaving the train free to continue its journey by crossing to the S & D single line section to Blandford at B.

Apart from these two trains all other trains which entered Templecombe from the S & D line needed a pilot if they had to 'reverse' in or out of the station. This even includes the 2-set on the 3.35 pm (SX during the summer service) Templecombe to Bailey Gate. The Bailey Gate train was something of an odd man out to Templecombe services, rather like the 6.05 pm Binegar train was to services out of Bath. The stock of the 3.35 pm, as mentioned in Chapter 8, arrived as part of the 9.45 am from Highbridge shortly after 11.00 am. The run down to Bailey Gate was mainly to collect full milk tanks for return to Templecombe, although the train did form a useful connection for passengers off the 1.00 pm express from Waterloo. The milk tanks were worked up to London from Templecombe over the Exeter to Waterloo main line. Normal motive power on the Bailey Gate train was an Ivatt 2-6-2T but 57XX pannier tanks, BR Standard class 3 2-6-2Ts, 3F 0-6-0 tender engines and 22XXs have also been seen on this duty. In 1960, the Stanier class 3 2-6-2Ts worked the service on occasions. The return working was due back in Templecombe shortly after 6.00 pm.

Pilot engines most frequently used over the years were the 3Fs, although others were drawn from a mixed bag to include pannier tanks, Ivatt 2-6-2Ts and BR Standard class 3 2-6-2Ts amongst others. The 0-8-0T Z class loco, 30953, and the 0-6-0T G6 class loco, 30274, can also be added to the list of locos seen on the S & D. Although they had one daily pilot duty, the 9.53 am from Bath, their main job was shunting in the Upper yard.

Freight services thinned out considerably south of Templecombe. Freights running in 1961 were the Up and Down Mail (the *Pines* loco diagram, SX during the summer service), the 6.35 am Evercreech Junction to Poole and 3.03 pm return to Templecombe, a return trip freight to Blandford Forum, and a MO Q engine and brake van to Sturminster Newton. This last train was in connection with market

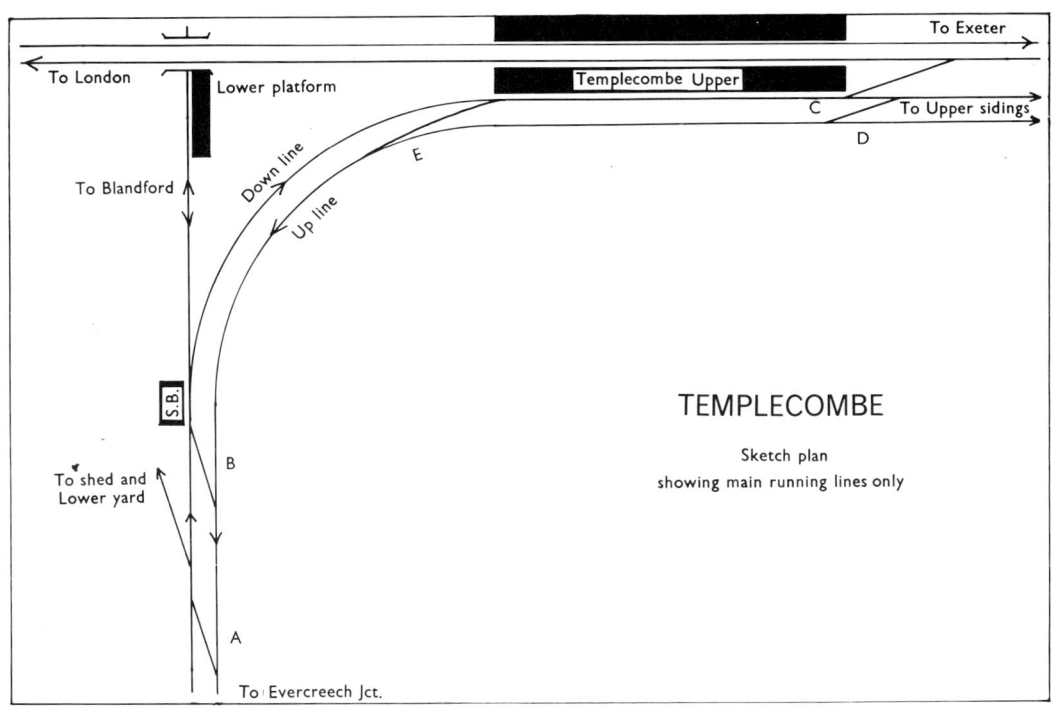

day at Sturminster Newton and was run to get cattle wagons to and from Templecombe.

All summer 1961 weekday passenger trains were booked to call at Templecombe Upper with the exception of the Up and Down *Pines* and the 11.40 am Bournemouth West to Bristol Temple Meads. (The 11.40 am Up, however, was booked to stop at the Lower platform for crew changing only). The weekday services to Templecombe mentioned in the timetables in the appendix were supplemented south by trains at 7.35 am and 12.23 pm to Bournemouth West, with trains arriving back from Bournemouth West at 11.01 am and 7.01 pm, not forgetting the return trip of the 2-set to and from Bailey Gate. The 11.01 am arrival formed an important connecting service with the Up *Pines Express* at Stalbridge. The method by which the connection was made is detailed within the next chapter. One train did terminate at Templecombe Lower platform. In 1961 that was the 10.00 pm SO from Bournemouth West arriving at 11.17 pm. The loco and stock then went direct to the Lower yard for disposal. The engine shed, turntable and coaling facilities at Templecombe were situated in the Lower yard. The hoist and bucket method of coaling used would make an interesting item to model.

Below *BR Standard class 4 4-6-0, 75071, is about to pass through Templecombe Lower platform and under the Southern Region main line from Waterloo to Exeter with a Bristol to Bournemouth West train on June 28 1962* (Derek Cross).

Right *The 3.35 pm Templecombe to Bailey Gate descends the bank from Templecombe Upper to No 2 Junction piloted by BR Standard class 3 2-6-2T, 82002, on June 28 1962. The stock is a B set with another Standard class 3 tank loco at the head. Templecombe Lower yard and engine shed are in the left of the picture. The turnout seen in front of 82002 leads to the S & D line towards Blandford Forum* (Derek Cross).

Below right *The Down* Pines Express *enters the single track section of the line from Templecombe No 2 Junction on June 28 1962, headed by 9F 2-10-0, 92233* (Derek Cross).

Templecombe 85

Above *9F 2-10-0, 92245, passes Templecombe shed with a Bournemouth West to Bristol Temple Meads train of three coaches and two vans on June 28 1962. Visible on shed are 3F 0-6-0, 43216, and BR Standard class 4 4-6-0, 75023* (Derek Cross).

Below *A 22XX class loco being coaled by hoist and bucket at Templecombe shed* (Roy Bullock).

Above *A Highbridge to Templecombe train behind 22XX class, 3215, has authority to take the road for Templecombe Upper on June 28 1962* (Derek Cross).

Below *4F 0-6-0, 44558, heads for Templecombe Upper with a freight on June 28 1962. Notice the freight train headlamp code* (Derek Cross).

Chapter 10

The rest of the line to Bournemouth West

The fact that the rest of the line down to Bournemouth West is being dealt with under one chapter should not be misread as meaning that it is any less important or interesting. The reason for this treatment is that most freight trains ran between Bath and Evercreech Junction. Consequently, there is a degree of extra diversity of operation and operation is fundamentally the main subject of this book.

From Templecombe the line was now single track down to Blandford Forum, with passing loops at three stations: Stalbridge, Sturminster Newton and Shillingstone. These passing loops enabled Up trains to pass straight through, whilst Down trains had to slow down to go through the loops. There was no facility to make the Up line bi-directional at slack times, a fact no doubt regretted by many a crew of a Down train when trying to make up lost time. All the stations between Templecombe and Blandford Forum, namely Henstridge, Stalbridge, Sturminster Newton, Shillingstone and Stourpaine & Durweston Halt, are eminently suitable for modelling purposes. They were all fairly small affairs but, of course, saw the majority of holiday trains and other traffic which could be seen elsewhere on the S & D line.

Stalbridge, in particular, was the setting for an interesting manoeuvre on weekdays. In 1961, the 8.55 am Bournemouth West to Templecombe local train arrived in the Up platform at 10.18 am. Passengers who had boarded the train along the line, and who wished to join the following *Pines Express*, would disembark from the 8.55 am, leaving the Henstridge and Templecombe passengers still sitting in the train. The train then moved forward up the single line as far as necessary to clear the turnout into the loop. The signalman set the road for the train to reverse into the Down platform. The Up *Pines Express* then arrived in the vacated Up platform at 10.39 am, subsequently departing at 10.41 am. Once the express had cleared the section, the 8.55 am reversed back out of the Down platform to regain the single line at the south end of the station. The signalman set the road for the Up platform and the 8.55 am arrived in the station for the second time in the day. Departure to Henstridge and Templecombe Upper was at 10.47 am.

Double track was regained on entering Blandford Forum station, continuing through Charlton Marshall Halt which, like Stourpaine & Durweston Halt, was closed in September 1956. The line continued south through Spetisbury (also closed in 1956) to arrive at Bailey Gate. This station would make an operationally interesting model, with milk traffic in and out of the sidings. This traffic was usually handled by the return working of the 3.35 pm SX from Templecombe, at 4.41 pm. On summer Saturdays, when trains were running late or out of sequence, it was sometimes difficult to find paths for all trains. This situation occasionally resulted in the milk train being combined with the 3.40 pm Bournemouth West to Bristol Temple Meads. As the 3.35 pm from Templecombe did not run on Saturdays, an engine and van would go down to Bailey Gate from Templecombe shortly after 2.00 pm. The combination of the trains was effected by this engine pulling the tanks out of the dairy siding and attaching them to the rear of the 3.40 pm. The loco then ran round the combined trains and coupled ahead of the passenger train loco. The method by which vans concerned with watercress traffic

The rest of the line

were shunted to the Up siding for storage at Bailey Gate is described in Peter Smith's book, *Mendips Engineman*. The shunting of Carter's siding is also described.

At Corfe Mullen Junction the line reverted to single track down to Broadstone Junction where the story really ends as far as this book is concerned. The line continued over ex-Southern Railway metals for the final eight miles through Poole, Parkstone and Branksome to Bournemouth West. For those who like to model loco sheds, Branksome depot would make an ideal subject. Although it was comparatively small, the range of loco classes which could be seen there on summer Saturdays was extremely varied.

Below *The 3.40 pm Bournemouth West to Bristol Temple Meads leaving Broadstone in April 1962. The loco, Stanier Black 5, 44963, is a 'foreigner' from Saltley (21A) that Bath shed has borrowed for a return trip over the S & D* (Malcolm Lewis).

Bottom *BR Standard class 4 4-6-0, 75073, about to leave Bournemouth West with the 3.40 pm to Bristol Temple Meads on February 17 1962* (Roy Bullock).

Chapter 11

Conclusions

By the time this book appears in print the renovation of the station buildings at Bath (Green Park) will be completed and a supermarket will stand near the point where locos once coupled up to the stock of the *Pines Express* and many other unnamed, but nonetheless important, trains. The credit goes to J. Sainsbury Ltd, in association with Bath City Council, for refurbishing these historic buildings to such a high standard.

Many people have photographed trains on the S & D. A great number of those photographs appear in the books listed at the end of this chapter. The sound of the line has also been perpetuated on record and cassette. To hear the combination of a Class 2P 4-4-0 and a Standard class 5 ascending Devonshire Bank or the Mendip Hills, is something that should not be missed if one is to fully appreciate what the S & D was all about.

This work has concentrated on the period 1950 to 1966. If the reader wishes to delve back further into history or make a more intensive study of certain periods then there are at least two options available. The first is to visit the Public Record Office, Ruskin Avenue, Kew, Richmond, Surrey. A wealth of information can be found there. For example, working timetables back to 1875 and 1876 are available for inspection and photocopies can be obtained. The early working timetables even include a list of fines and punishments imposed upon staff members for various 'misdemeanours' during the currency of the previous timetable! The reference number RAIL 972/1 will find these timetables, whilst RAIL 1134/477 gives access to the 1904 Rule Book. The staff at the Office are most helpful, but a word of warning. Allow a good half a day to get used to the system employed or make some telephone enquiries before you go. It should also be remembered that working timetables do not always tell the full story.

Further information of all kinds relating to the S & D can be found at the Somerset and Dorset Railway Trust Museum. This is currently housed in the station at Washford on the West Somerset Railway line between Bishops Lydeard and Minehead. Details of opening times and dates can be found by referring to editions of the S & D Railway Trust *Bulletin*, published bi-monthly and obtainable from the Trust at Washford. Any of the books I have listed will help to give a complete picture of how the line rose to and fell from fortune. Some of the locos which actually ran over the line have been preserved, such as 9F 92220, *Evening Star*, 7Fs 53808 and 53809, Standard class 5, 73050, and Standard class 4 4-6-0, 75027. In fact, a representative of virtually every class which ran on the S & D has been preserved.

Finally, a few words of thanks to the people without whom this work would not have been possible. First and foremost my thanks go to Ivo Peters for the inspiration he gave me at the early stages of thought and planning. Indeed, it is to him that I wish to dedicate this work as a way of saying 'thank you'. An equal share of thanks go to Peter Smith, Peter Pike and Mike Arlett for checking my manuscript so diligently and giving such generous help and advice, often at very short notice. Richard Strange and his colleagues within the Mangotsfield Railway Circle are to be thanked for their help with intricate details of summer Saturday workings, along with Giles Tatton-Brown. For photographs I am indebted to Ivo Peters, Peter Pike, Malcolm Lewis, R.E. Toop, Roy Bullock, R.C. Riley,

G. Richardson and Derek Cross and for other information I thank Colin Penfold, Bruce Wright, Michael Jennings, Mike Buckingham and the officers and members of the S & D Railway Trust. Last, but by no means least, a special word of thanks to my wife, Anne, for typing and re-typing the manuscript so well.

Bibliography

The Somerset and Dorset (An English Cross Country Railway), Ivo Peters, Oxford Publishing Co.
The Somerset and Dorset in the Fifties Volume 1, Ivo Peters, Oxford Publishing Co.
The Somerset and Dorset in the Fifties Volume 2, Ivo Peters, Oxford Publishing Co.
Historical Survey of the Somerset and Dorset Railway, C.W. Judge/C.R. Potts, Oxford Publishing Co.
Mendips Engineman, P.W. Smith, Oxford Publishing Co.
Footplate over the Mendips, P.W. Smith, Oxford Publishing Co.
Somerset and Dorset Engineman, F.E. Stickley, Oakwood Press.
Steam on the Somerset and Dorset, G.A. Richardson, Bradford Barton.
S & D Working Timebook 1920/1931, Oxford Publishing Co.
S & D Working Timetable 1950, Oxford Publishing Co.
Highbridge in its heyday, C. Maggs, Oakwood Press.
The Bridgwater Branch, J.D. Harrison, Oakwood Press.
Picture History of the Somerset and Dorset, R. Atthill, David & Charles Ltd.
The Somerset and Dorset, R. Atthill, David & Charles Ltd.
Somerset and Dorset Locomotive History, D. Brackley/D. Milton, David & Charles Ltd.
The Somerset and Dorset Railway, Barrie and Clinker, Oakwood Press.
The Railways and Tramways of Radstock, C. Handley, S & D Trust.
The Somerset and Dorset 2-8-0s, D. Milton, S & D Trust.
PSL Model Railway Guides 1-8, M. Andress, Patrick Stephens Ltd.
How to go Railway Modelling, N. Simmons, Patrick Stephens Ltd.

Appendices

Appendix A

Working timetable Bath (Green Park), Monday to Friday, Midsummer 1961

Train arriving from		Pla	arr am	dep am	Train departing to
11.03 pm	MX. Ft. Avonmouth	—	1.00	—	
8.10 pm	Ft. Poole	—	1.14	—	
1.02 am	MX. Ft. Westerleigh	—	1.45	—	
		—	—	2.30	MX. Ft. Westerleigh
11.53 pm	Q. Ft. Templecombe	N	2.39	—	
		—	—	2.40	Ft. & Mail. Poole/B. West
		—	—	3.30	Ft. Evercreech Jct.
		—	—	3.50	MX. Ft. Clifton Bridge
		—	—	4.50	MO. Ft. Westerleigh
4.20 am	MX. Ft. Westerleigh	—	4.57	—	
		—	—	5.00	Ft. Evercreech Jct.
		—	—	5.30	Ft. Westerleigh
		—	—	5.50	Ft. Templecombe
12.37 am	MX. Pcls. Leicester	S	6.03	—	
		—	—	6.20	Bristol T M
5.58 am	Bristol T M	N	6.38	6.48	Bournemouth West
		N	—	7.01	Bristol T M
		N	—	7.23	Bristol T M
		N	—	7.25	Q. Ft. Co-op sidings
7.10 am	Bristol T M	N	7.49	—	
8.00 am	Q. Ft. Co-op sidings	—	8.10	—	
		—	—	8.11	Bristol T M
		—	—	8.15	Templecombe
7.45 am	Bristol T M	N	8.22	—	
7.00 am	Templecombe	S	8.42	—	
		—	—	8.55	Ft. Midsomer Norton
8.20 am	Ft. Westerleigh	—	9.20	—	
9.03 am	Bristol T M	S	9.48	9.53	Bournemouth West
6.25 am	Ft. Evercreech Jct.	N	9.50	—	
		—	—	10.10	Bristol T M
8.00 am	Ft. Evercreech Jct.	—	10.25	—	
7.33 am	Broadstone	—	10.46	—	
		—	—	11.00	Ft. Evercreech Jct.
10.40 am	Ft. Midsomer Norton	—	11.21	—	
9.45 am	B. West (Pines)	S	11.56	12.01	Manchester (Pines)

Train arriving from		Pla	arr pm	dep pm	Train departing to
6.05 am	Ft. Templecombe	—	12.23	—	
11.49 am	Bristol T M	N	12.26	12.35	Ft. Midsomer Norton
		—	—	1.00	Ft. Westerleigh
12.20 pm	EBV. Stapleton Rd.	N	1.02	1.10	Templecombe
12.00 pm	Templecombe	N	1.35	—	
11.40 am	Bournemouth West	S	1.53	2.00	Bristol T M
		—	—	2.00	Ft. Evercreech Jct.
1.50 pm	Ft. Midsomer Norton	—	2.31	2.40	Ft. Westerleigh
10.30 am	Manchester (Pines)	S	3.03	3.09	B. West (Pines)
		—	—	3.20	Templecombe
2.40 pm	Ft. Westerleigh	—	3.25	—	
3.25 pm	MX. L/E. Westerleigh	—	3.55	—	
3.35 pm	Bristol T M	N	4.12	4.21	Bournemouth West
1.10 pm	Bournemouth West	S	4.22	4.30	Bristol T M
		—	—	4.37	Templecombe
1.50 pm	Ft. Evercreech Jct.	S	5.10	—	
5.06 pm	Bristol T M	S	5.44	5.45	Bristol T M
		—	—	6.05	Binegar
4.15 pm	Templecombe	N	6.00	6.18	Bristol T M
5.44 pm	Bristol T M	S	6.23	6.27	FX. Ft. Westerleigh
6.02 pm	Bristol T M	N	6.40	7.05	Bournemouth West
3.40 pm	Bournemouth West	S	6.56	7.03	Bristol T M
6.55 pm	Bristol T M	N	7.39	8.00	L/E. Lawrence Hill Jct.
7.10 pm	Binegar	—	8.03	—	
7.10 pm	Ft. Westerleigh	—	8.25	—	
7.20 pm	Ft. Evercreech Jct.	—	8.48	—	
8.10 pm	Bristol T M	—	8.50	8.55	Q. Ft. Templecombe
		—	—	9.15	Ft. Birmingham
8.25 pm	Perish. Templecombe	S	9.58	10.15	Derby
6.48 pm	Bournemouth West	N	10.21	10.25	Templecombe
		—	—	11.29	Ft. Westerleigh

Appendix B

Working timetable Bath (Green Park), Saturdays only, Midsummer 1961

Train arriving from		Pla	arr am	dep am	Train departing to
10.20 pm	Ft. Avonmouth	—	12.05	—	
8.10 pm	Ft. Poole	—	1.14	—	
1.02 am	Ft. Westerleigh	—	1.45	—	
10.00 pm	Fri. Sheffield	S	2.25	2.35	Bournemouth West
		—	—	2.30	Ft. Westerleigh
11.53 pm	Q. Ft. Templecombe	—	2.39	—	
		N	—	2.40	Mails. Poole
8.25 pm	Fri. Bradford	S	2.55	3.15	Bournemouth West
10.28 pm	Fri. Manchester	S	3.45	4.10	Bournemouth West
		—	—	4.50	Ft. Westerleigh
4.20 am	Ft. Westerleigh	—	4.57	—	
		N	—	6.20	Bristol T M
12.37 am	Pcls. Leicester	S	6.27	—	
5.58 am	Bristol T M	S	6.38	6.48	Bournemouth West
		N	—	7.01	Bristol T M
		N	—	7.23	Bristol T M
7.10 am	Bristol T M	N	7.49	—	
		N	—	8.11	Bristol T M
		N	—	8.15	Templecombe
7.45 am	Bristol T M	N	8.22	—	
7.00 am	Templecombe	N	8.42	—	
9.03 am	Bristol T M	N	9.48	9.53	Bournemouth West
		N	—	10.10	Bristol T M
8.00 am	Q. Bournemouth West	N	10.14	10.25	Relief
7.43 am	Birmingham	S	10.20	10.32	Bournemouth West
8.16 am	Q. Bournemouth West	N	10.31	10.45	Relief
7.12 am	Bournemouth West	N	10.59	—	
8.40 am	Bournemouth West	N	11.14	11.25	Bradford
9.08 am	Birmingham	N	11.39	12.00	Bournemouth West
9.25 am	Bournemouth West	S	11.45	11.50	Liv/Manchester
9.45 am	B. West (Pines)	S	11.56	12.05	Manchester (Pines)

Train arriving from		Pla	arr pm	dep pm	Train departing to
7.35 am	Nottingham	N	12.05	12.24	Bournemouth West
		S	—	12.20	Bristol T M
9.55 am	Bournemouth West	S	12.25	12.35	Leeds
10.05 am	Bournemouth West	S	12.45	12.50	Derby
12.12 pm	Bristol T M	N	12.49	—	
10.32 am	Bournemouth West	S	1.00	1.05	Manchester
		S	—	1.10	Templecombe
12.50 pm	L/E. Westerleigh	—	1.20	—	
12.03 pm	Templecombe	N	1.35	—	
11.12 am	Bournemouth West	N	1.49	1.55	Sheffield
7.00 am	Cleethorpes	S	2.02	2.12	Exmouth
		—	—	2.05	Bristol T M
10.40 am	Exmouth	N	2.10	2.18	Cleethorpes
9.35 am	Sheffield	S	2.15	2.30	Bournemouth West
1.45 pm	Bristol T M	S	2.24	—	
12.00 pm	Bournemouth West	S	2.34	2.45	Relief
7.43 am	Bradford	S	2.47	2.52	Bournemouth West
12.20 pm	Bournemouth West	S	2.54	3.05	Nottingham
2.29 pm	Bristol T M	N	3.11	—	
10.30 am	Manchester (Pines)	S	3.25	3.30	B. West (Pines)
10.55 am	Manchester	S	3.52	4.21	Bournemouth West
3.30 pm	Bristol T M	N	4.07	—	
1.10 pm	Bournemouth West	S	4.22	4.30	Bristol T M
		S	—	4.37	Templecombe
4.52 pm	Bristol T M	S	5.39	5.45	Bristol T M
4.15 pm	Templecombe	N	6.00	—	
		—	—	6.18	Bristol T M
		—	—	6.27	Ft. Avonmouth
6.08 pm	Bristol T M	S	6.47	7.05	Bournemouth West
3.40 pm	Bournemouth West	S	6.56	7.03	Bristol T M
6.15 pm	Ft. Bristol	—	7.15	—	
6.55 pm	Bristol T M	N	7.39	—	
8.10 pm	Bristol T M	—	8.50	—	
		—	—	9.15	Ft. Birmingham
7.25 pm	Bournemouth West	S	9.53	9.58	Bristol T M
		N	—	10.08	Bristol T M
		N	—	10.20	Ft. Bristol
6.48 pm	Bournemouth West	N	10.21	10.25	Templecombe
		S	—	11.29	Ft. Westerleigh

Appendix C

Down line, Monday to Saturday, Midsummer 1961

Midford		Radstock		Midsomer Norton		Binegar			Train	
arr	dep	arr	dep	arr	dep	arr	dep			
am		am		am		am				
2.45		2.55		—		—		SO	10.00 pm	Fri. Sheffield–B. West
3.05		3.16		3.23		3.37		SO	2.40 am	Mail. Bath–Poole
3.07		3.23		3.32		3.52		SX	2.40 am	Ft. and Mail. Bath–B. West
3.25		3.35		—		—		SO	8.25 am	Fri. Bradford–B. West
3.45		4.05 A 4.08		4.18		4.38		SO	3.30 am	Ft. Bath–Evercreech Jct.
4.20		4.30		—		—		SO	10.28 pm	Fri. Manchester–B. West
5.15		5.35 A 5.38		5.48		6.08		SX	5.00 am	Ft. Bath–Templecombe
6.05	6.20	6.57	7.40	7.50	8.00	8.55 S 9.26		SX	5.50 am	Ft. Bath–Evercreech Jct.
6.59	7.00	7.15	7.19	7.25	7.30	7.45	7.46		8.15 am	Bristol T M–B. West
8.26	8.27	8.43	8.44	8.50	8.51	9.06	9.07			Bath–Templecombe
9.12		—		9.45		—		SX	8.55 am	Ft. Bath–Midsomer N.
10.05		10.16 10.18		10.24 10.29		—		T	9.03 am	Bristol T M–B. West
10.42		10.51		—		—		SO	7.43 am	Birmingham–B. West
				11.50 12.10		—		SX	11.00 am	Ft. Bath–Evercreech Jct.
pm		pm		pm		pm				
12.10		12.20		—		—		SO	9.08 am	Birmingham–B. West
12.34		12.45		—		—		SO	7.35 am	Nottingham–B. West
12.52		—		—		—		SX	12.35 pm	Ft. Bath–Midsomer N
1.21	1.22	1.12 A 1.15	1.39	1.27	1.46	2.01	2.02		1.10 pm	Bath–Templecombe
		1.37	1.55	1.45				SX	1.55 pm	L/E Radstock–Midsomer N.
2.15		2.35 A 2.38		2.00		—		SX	2.00 pm	Ft. Bath–Evercreech Jct.
2.22		2.32		2.48		3.08		SO	7.00 am	Cleethorpes–Exmouth
2.40		2.49		—		—		SO	9.35 am	Sheffield–B. West
3.02		3.11		—		—		SO	7.43 am	Bradford–B. West
3.19		3.28		—		—		SX	10.30 am	Manchester–B. West (Pines)
3.31	3.32	3.48	3.50	3.57	3.59	4.14	4.15		3.20 pm	Bath–Templecombe
3.40		3.49		—		—		SO	10.30 am	Manchester–B. West (Pines)
4.31		4.39		—		—		SO	10.55 am	Manchester–B. West
4.31		4.39		—		—		SX	3.35 pm	Bristol T M–B. West
4.48	4.49	5.05	5.06	5.13	5.17	5.32	5.33		4.37 pm	Bath–Templecombe
6.16	6.17	6.33	6.34	6.41	6.42	6.57	—	SX	6.05 pm	Bath–Binegar
7.16	7.17	7.32	7.34	7.40	7.42	7.57	7.58		6.02 pm	Bristol T M–B. West
		9.28		—		—		SX	8.55 pm	Q. Ft. Bath–Templecombe
10.36	10.38	10.58	10.59	11.06	11.08	11.24	11.25		10.25 pm	Bath–Templecombe

S = Shunts for train to pass.
T = Stops at Midford on Thursdays.
A = Stops to attach banker.
W = Stops to take water.

Appendix D

Up line, Monday to Saturday, Midsummer 1961

Binegar		Midsomer Norton		Radstock		Midford			Train	
arr	dep	arr	dep	arr	dep	arr	dep			
am		am		am		am				
1.51		2.04		2.10		2.23		SX	11.53 pm	Q. Ft. Templecombe–Bath (Banked 3.30 am Ft.)
	4.45			5.05		—		SX	L/E	Ft. Evercreech Jct.–Bath
7.13	8.07	8.55	9.15	9.22		9.35		SX	6.25 am	Templecombe–Bath
7.59	8.00	8.10	8.11	8.15	8.16	8.31	8.32	SX	7.00 am	Ft. Evercreech Jct.–Bath
8.48 D 9.30		—	9.45	9.53		10.10		SX	8.00 am	Templecombe–Bath
10.38		10.52	11.10	11.18	11.50	12.08		SO	6.05 am	Ft. Templecombe–Bath
	9.48				9.56	10.05		SO	8.00 am	Q. B. West–Relief
	10.00				10.08	10.17 F 10.22		SX	8.16 am	Q. B. West–Relief
10.04	10.05	10.14	10.15	10.19	10.20	10.36	10.37	SO	7.33 am	Broadstone–Bath
10.18	10.19	10.26	10.28	10.32	10.33	10.48	10.49	SO	7.12 am	B. West–Bath
—		—	10.40	10.47		11.04		SX	10.40 am	Ft. Midsomer N.–Bath
10.48		—		10.56		11.05		SO	8.40 am	B. West–Bradford
11.18		—		11.26		11.35		SO	9.25 am	B. West–Liv/Manchester
11.29		—		11.37		11.46		SX	9.45 am	B. West–Manchester (Pines)
11.51		—		11.59		12.09 X 12.15		SX	9.55 am	B. West–Leeds
pm		pm		pm		pm				
12.13		—		12.22		12.31 X 12.36		SO	10.05 am	B. West–Derby
12.34		—		12.42		12.51		SO	10.32 am	B. West–Manchester
12.52	12.53	1.02	1.03	1.07	1.08	1.25	1.26	SO	12.00 pm	Templecombe–Bath
12.55	12.56	1.05	1.06	1.10	1.11	1.26	1.27	SX	12.03 pm	Templecombe–Bath
	1.12				1.21 F 1.30	1.40		SX	11.12 am	B. West–Sheffield
	1.27				1.35	1.44		SO	11.40 am	B. West–Bristol T M
	1.36				1.45	1.55 F 2.00		SO	10.40 am	Exmouth–Cleethorpes
—		—	1.50	1.57		2.14		SX	1.50 pm	Ft. Midsomer N.–Bath
	1.53				2.02	2.12 X 2.24		SO	12.00 pm	B. West–Relief
	2.29				2.36	2.45		SO	12.20 pm	B. West–Nottingham
2.36 D 2.46		3.05	3.20	3.32 S 4.02		4.25 X 4.50		SX	1.50 pm	Ft. Evercreech Jct.–Bath
3.37	3.38	3.48	3.49	3.53	3.55	4.11	4.12	SX	1.10 pm	B. West–Bristol T M
	3.45				4.15	—		SX	L/E	(After banking 2pm. Bath Ft.) Templecombe–Bath
5.15	5.16	5.26	5.28	5.32	5.34	5.49	5.50		4.15 pm	B. West–Bristol T M
	6.25	6.31	6.32	6.36	6.38	6.47		SX	3.40 pm	Binegar–Bath
	7.10	7.23	7.29	7.33	7.34	7.49	7.53		7.10 pm	Ft. Evercreech Jct.–Bath
8.01		8.14		8.20		8.33		SO	7.20 pm	B. West–Bristol T M
9.19		9.27	9.28	9.33	9.34	9.44		SO	7.25 pm	Perish. T/Combe–Derby
	9.28				9.38	9.48		SX	8.25 pm	B. West–Bath
9R45		9.53	9.54	9.59	10.00	10R11			6.48 pm	B. West–Relief
12.18 D 12.20		12.35		12.42		12.59		SX	8.10 pm	Ft. Poole–Bath
1.13 D 1.16		1.31		1.38		1.55		SU	9.15 pm	Sat. Ft. Poole–Bath

D = Stops to detach assisting engine.
X = Crosses another train. (Train waits at 'outer home' signal on double track).
S = Shunts for train to pass.
R = Stops when required.
F = Stops for working purposes only. Stop not made if running late.

Appendix E

Evercreech Junction. Up and Down lines, Monday to Friday, Midsummer 1961

Up

North Sidings arr	North Sidings dep	Station arr	Station dep	Up Sidings arr	Up Sidings dep	Train	
am	am	am	am	am	am		
—	—	12.25 W 12.33	1.10	12.42	1.10	11.53 pm	Q. Ft. Templecombe—Bath
—	—	4.39 W 4.50	—	4.52	—	2.40 am	Ft. and Mail. Bath—B. West
—	—	—	—	5.01	6.05	4.20 am	MO. L/E from Templecombe
—	—	4.52 W 4.57	—	—	—	4.20 am	Ft. Templecombe—Highbridge
5.30	—	—	—	6.20	—	3.30 am	Ft. From Bath
—	—	—	—	—	6.25	6.00 am	L/E from Templecombe
—	6.35	6.44 W 6.55	—	—	—		Ft. To Bath
—	—	—	—	—	—		Ft. To Poole
—	—	6.51 W 7.00	—	7.09	8.30	6.05 am	Ft. Templecombe—Bath
7.15	—	—	—	—	—	5.00 am	Ft. From Bath
—	—	—	8.00	—	—		Ft. To Bath
—	—	7.23	7.25	—	—	7.00 am	Templecombe—Bath
—	—	7.56	—	—	—	7.00 am	From Highbridge
—	—	8.05	8.14	—	—	5.58 am	Bristol T M—B. West
—	—	—	8.15	—	—		To Highbridge
—	8.30	—	8.32	—	—		L/E to Templecombe
—	—	8.46	—	—	—	8.20 am	From Templecombe
—	—	9.28	9.30	—	—	7.33 am	Broadstone—Bath
—	—	9.28	9.32	—	—	8.15 am	Bath—Templecombe
—	—	—	9.55	—	—		To Highbridge
—	—	10.35	—	—	—		L/E from Templecombe. *Pines* pilot
10.35	11.40	—	11.49	—	—	5.50 am	Ft. Bath—Templecombe
—	—	10.43	—	—	—	10.20 am	From Templecombe
—	—	10.44	10.47	—	—	9.45 am	Highbridge—Templecombe
—	—	11.03	11.05	—	—	9.03 am	Bristol T M—B. West
—	—	11.03	11.06	—	—	9.45 am	B. West—Manchester (*Pnes*)
—	—	—	—	—	11.06		Ft. To Highbridge

Down

North Sidings arr	North Sidings dep	Station arr	Station dep	Up Sidings arr	Up Sidings dep	Train	
		pm	pm		pm		
—	—	12.20	12.21	—	—	12.00 pm	Templecombe—Bath
—	—	12.51	—	—	—	12.30 pm	ECS from Templecombe
1.02	—	—	—	—	—	7.38 am	Ft. From Highbridge
—	—	1.02	1.04	—	—	11.40 am	B. West—Bristol T M
1.10	—	—	1.15	—	—	11.00 am	Ft. From Bath
—	—	—	—	—	1.50		To Highbridge
—	—	—	—	2.07	—	1.15 pm	Ft. From Templecombe
—	—	2.24	2.27	—	—	1.10 pm	Bath—Templecombe
—	2.35	—	—	—	—		Ft. To Templecombe
—	—	3.04	3.06	—	—	1.10 pm	B. West—Bristol T M
—	—	3.19	3.24	—	—	2.20 pm	Highbridge—Templecombe
3.53	—	3.35	—	—	—	3.15 pm	L/E from Templecombe
—	—	—	—	—	—	2.00 pm	Ft. From Bath
—	—	—	—	—	4.00		Ft. To Evercreech New
—	—	4.05	4.10	—	—	10.30 am	Manchester—B. West (*Pines*)
—	—	—	4.16	—	—		To B. West
—	—	—	4.18	—	—		L/E to Templecombe. *Pines* pilot
—	—	4.29	—	—	—	4.05 pm	From Templecombe
—	—	4.38	4.40	—	—	3.20 pm	Bath—Templecombe
—	—	4.40	4.43	—	—	4.15 pm	Templecombe—Bath
4.45	—	—	—	—	—	4.35 pm	Ft. From Evercreech New
—	—	5.00	5.00	—	—	4.00 pm	From Highbridge
—	—	5.18	5.20	—	—	3.35 pm	Bristol T M—B. West
—	—	5.54 F	5.56	—	—	3.40 pm	B. West—Bristol T M
—	—	5.55	5.56	—	—	4.37 pm	Bath—Templecombe
—	—	—	F 6.02	—	—		To Highbridge
—	—	6.56	6.58	—	—	4.19 pm	Milk/Perish. Highbridge—T/Combe
—	—	6.46 W	6.52	7.01	—	5.38 pm	Ft. From Templecombe
—	—	—	—	—	7.20		Ft. To Bath
—	—	8.09	—	—	—	7.10 pm	From Highbridge
—	—	8.21	8.26	—	—	6.02 pm	Bristol T M—B. West
8.34	9.00	9.09 W	9.18	—	—	2.40 pm	Ft. Highbridge—Templecombe
—	—	8.47	9.04	—	—	8.25 pm	Perishables. Templecombe—Derby
—	—	9.13	9.15	—	—	6.48 pm	B. West—Bath
—	—	—	9.25	—	—		To Highbridge
—	—	10.30 W	10.40	—	—	8.55 pm	Q. Ft. Bath—Templecombe
—	—	10.46 W	10.56	11.05	11.30	8.10 pm	Ft. Poole—Bath
—	—	11.44 A	11.45	—	—	10.25 pm	Bath—Templecombe

W = Stops to take water.
F = Timings 2 minutes later on Fridays.
A = Approximate time only.

Appendix F

Evercreech Junction. Saturdays only, Midsummer 1961
With pilot, train loco and load details of certain trains on August 12 1961.

arr	dep	Train	Train	Pilot	Loco	Load
am						
3.32	3.37	10.00 pm	Fri. Sheffield—B. West		92001	
4.13	4.23	8.25 pm	Fri. Bradford—B. West		92006	
4.36	4.41	2.40 am	Mail. Bath—Poole		73054	
4.52 W	4.57	4.20 am	Ft. From Templecombe			
5.09	5.25	10.28 pm	Fri. Manchester—B. West		92000	
7.23	7.25	7.00 am	Templecombe—Bath			
7.56	—	7.00 am	From Highbridge			
8.05	8.14	5.58 am	Bristol T M—B. West		76027	
—	8.15		To Highbridge			
8.46	—	8.20 am	From Templecombe			
9.19	9.24	8.00 am	Q. B. West—Relief			
9.28	9.32	8.15 am	Bath—Templecombe			
9.30	9.36	8.16 am	Q. B. West—Relief			
9.41	9.43	7.12 am	B. West—Bath		75072	8 ECS
—	9.55		To Highbridge			
10.10	10.16	8.40 am	B. West—Bradford	40569	92001	11
10.35	—	10.15 am	L/E from Templecombe		40634	
10.44	10.47	9.45 am	Highbridge—Templecombe	40569	34045	12
10.49	10.54	9.25 am	B. West—Liv/Manchester	40634	92006	
11.01	11.06	9.45 am	B. West—Manchester (Pines)	40697	73047	
11.03	11.05	9.03 am	Bristol T M—B. West			
11.06	—		Ft. To Highbridge		92006	
11.16	11.23	9.55 am	B. West—Leeds		73051	8
11.29	11.33	7.43 am	Birmingham—B. West		73054	8
11.44	11.50	10.05 am	B. West—Derby	75027	73054	11
		pm				
12.01	12.06	10.32 am	B. West—Manchester	40697	34043	8
12.23	12.24	12.03 pm	Templecombe—Bath		75071	
12.39	12.45	11.12 am	B. West—Sheffield	40564	53810	10
12.51	—	12.30 pm	ECS. From Templecombe			
1.00	1.03	9.08 am	Birmingham—B. West	40700	73052	10
1.02	—	7.38 am	Ft. From Highbridge			
1.08	1.13	10.40 am	Exmouth—Cleethorpes	3210	53806	11
—	1.20		To Highbridge			
1.23	1.30	7.35 am	Nottingham—B. West		53807	10
1.24 A	1.30	12.00 pm	B. West—Relief (Kidsgrove)		73050	8
2.00	2.05	12.20 pm	B. West—Nottingham	40700	34041	10
2.24	2.27	1.10 pm	Bath—Templecombe		75072	
3.04	3.06	1.10 pm	B. West—Bristol T M		76027	
3.09	3.15	7.00 am	Cleethorpes—Exmouth	40569	44422	8
3.19	3.24	2.20 pm	Highbridge—Templecombe			
3.27	3.40	9.35 am	Sheffield—B. West		92001	10
3.28	—	3.05 pm	From Templecombe		75072	
3.50	3.57	7.43 am	Bradford—B. West		92006	10
—	4.16		To B. West			
4.26	4.31	10.30 am	Manchester—B. West (Pines)	40564	34045	12
4.29	—	4.05 pm	From Templecombe			
4.40	4.43	4.15 pm	Templecombe—Bath		44561	
—	5.00		To Highbridge			
5.00	5.10	4.00 pm	Highbridge—Templecombe			
5.18	5.20	10.55 am	Manchester—B. West	75027	34041	12
5.54	5.56	3.40 pm	B. West—Bristol T M		73047	
5.55	5.56	4.37 pm	Bath—Templecombe			
—	6.02		To B. West			
6.56	6.58	4.19 pm	Milk/Perish. H/Bridge—T/Combe			
8.09	—	7.10 pm	From Highbridge			
8.21	8.26	6.08 pm	Bristol T M—B. West		76027	
8.47	8.52	7.25 pm	B. West—Bristol T M		92006	
9.09 W	9.18	2.40 pm	Ft. Highbridge—Templecombe			
9.13	9.15	6.48 pm	B. West—Bath			
—	9.25		To Highbridge			
9.50	10.02	9.30 pm	Q. Milk. Templecombe—Highbridge		53807	
11.44 A	11.45	10.25 pm	Bath—Templecombe			
11.55	12.25	9.15 pm	Ft. Poole—Bath			

A = Approximate time only.
W = Stops to take water.